Girl

Faithful

Dr. Claus

DEDICATION

Christine Lauren

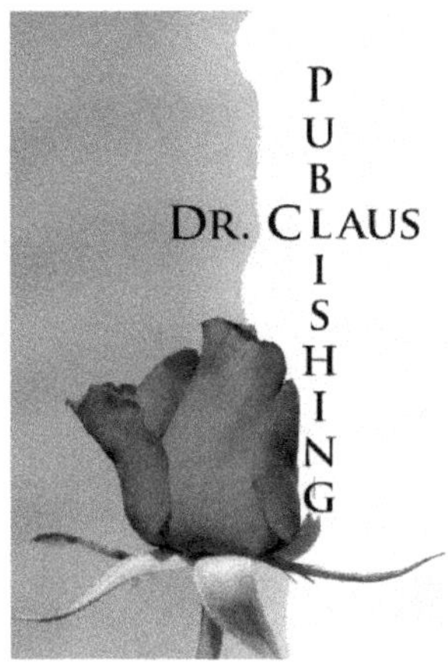

PUBLISHED BY DR. CLAUS PUBLISHING
Telford, Pa 18969

First Edition
ISBN: 1-61497-065-3
ISBN-13: 978-1-61497-065-1
Library of Congress Control Number: 2018911070

CONTENTS

ACKNOWLEDGMENTS

Love

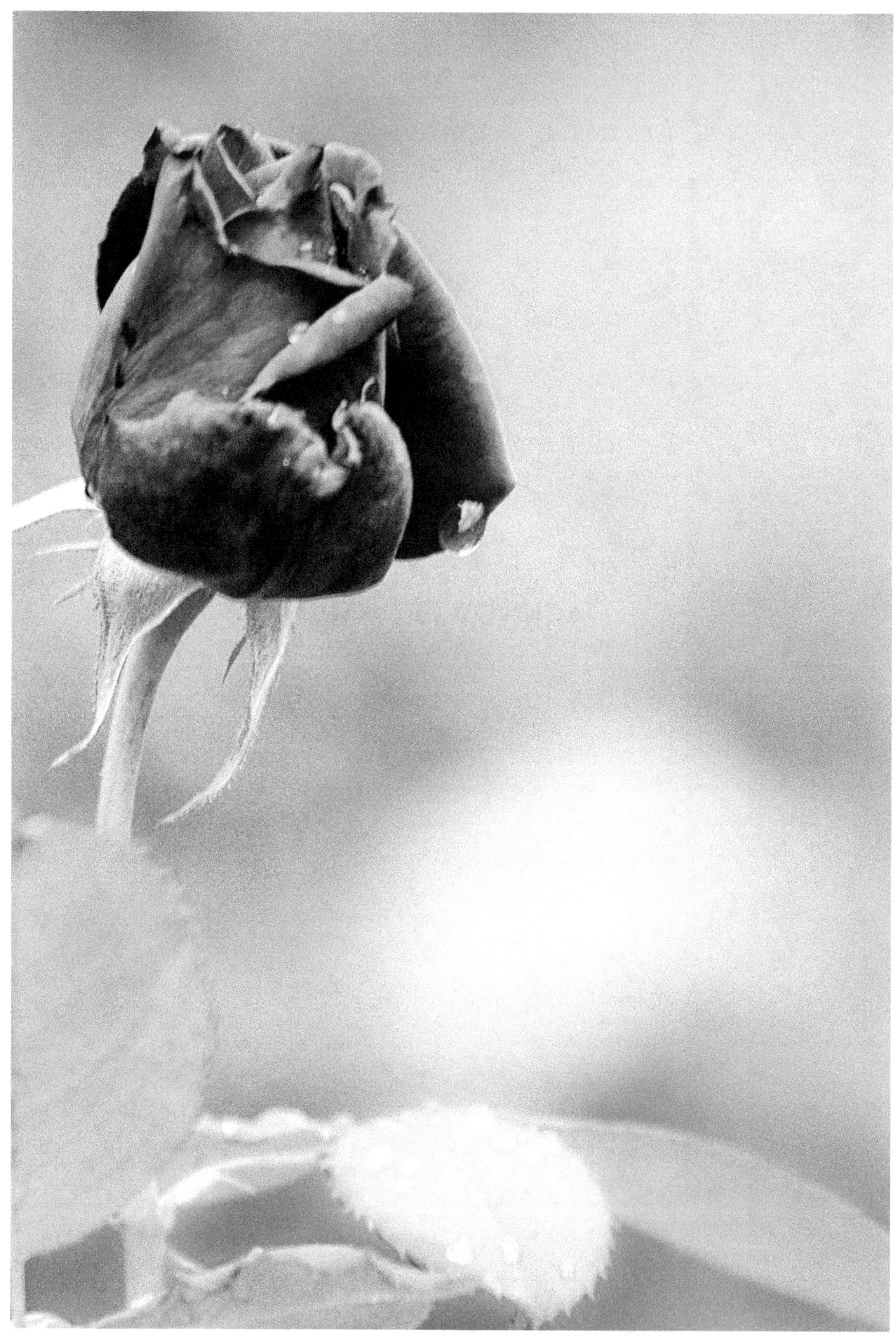

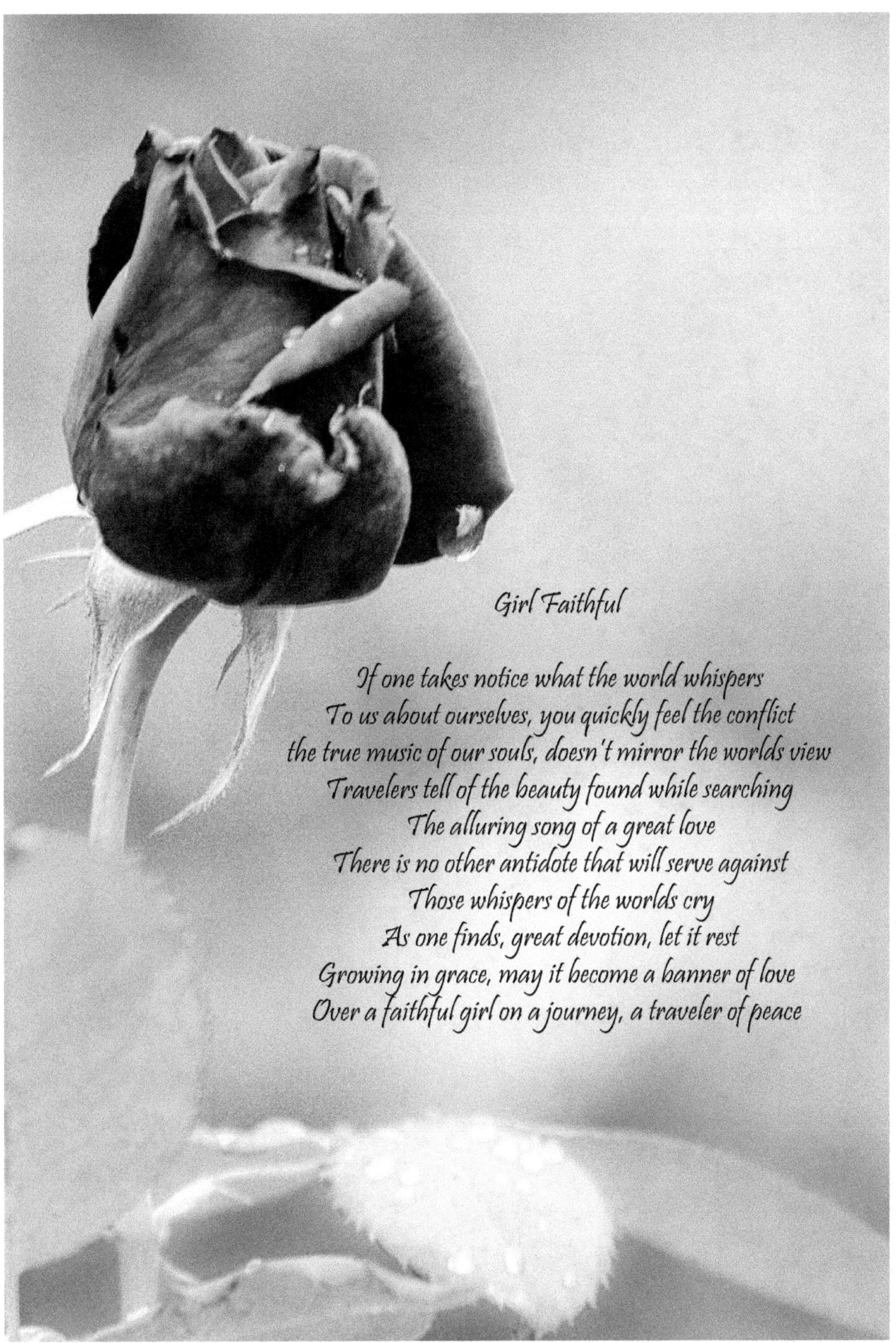

Girl Faithful

If one takes notice what the world whispers
To us about ourselves, you quickly feel the conflict
the true music of our souls, doesn't mirror the worlds view
Travelers tell of the beauty found while searching
The alluring song of a great love
There is no other antidote that will serve against
Those whispers of the worlds cry
As one finds, great devotion, let it rest
Growing in grace, may it become a banner of love
Over a faithful girl on a journey, a traveler of peace

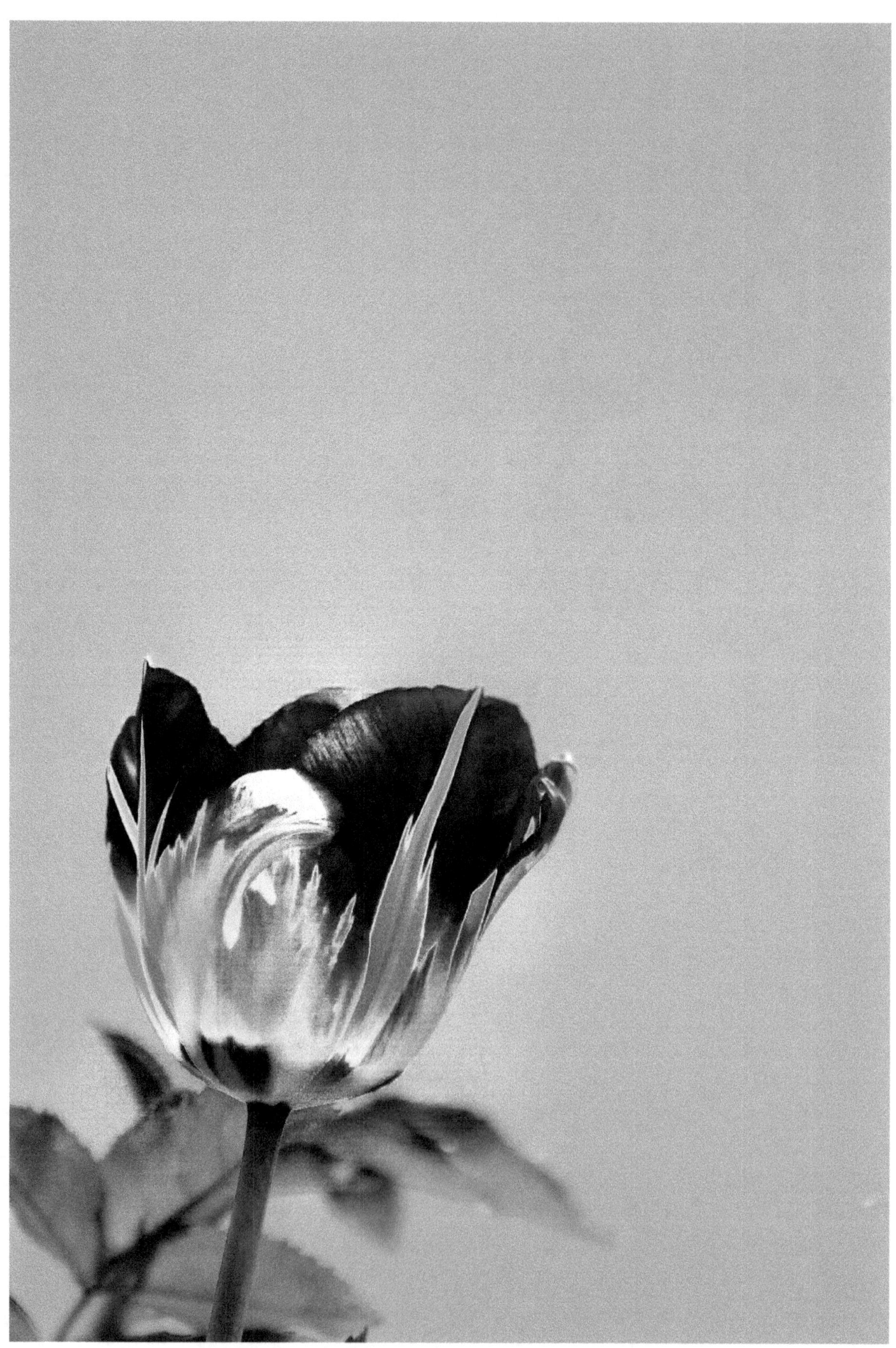

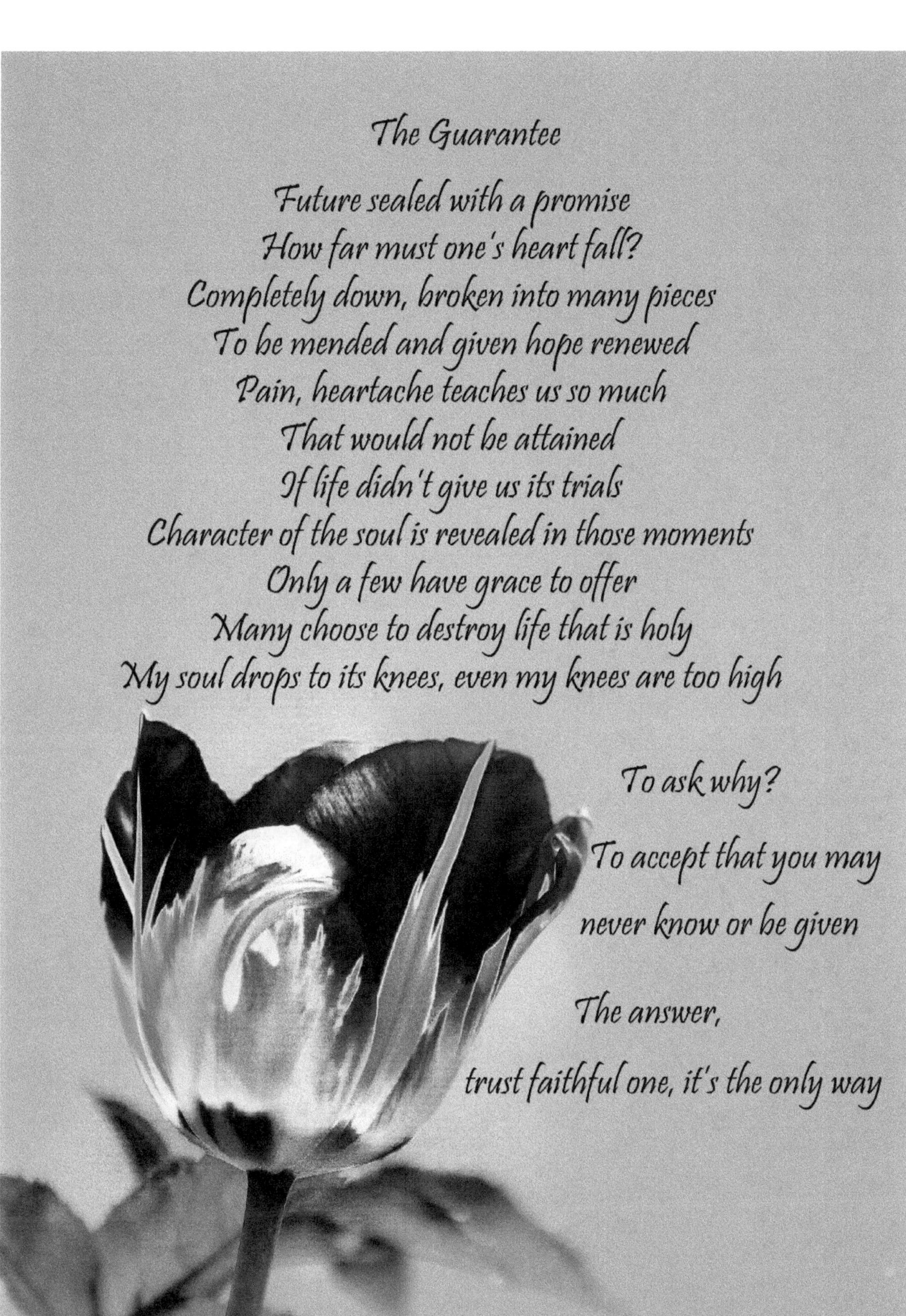

The Guarantee

Future sealed with a promise
How far must one's heart fall?
Completely down, broken into many pieces
To be mended and given hope renewed
Pain, heartache teaches us so much
That would not be attained
If life didn't give us its trials
Character of the soul is revealed in those moments
Only a few have grace to offer
Many choose to destroy life that is holy
My soul drops to its knees, even my knees are too high

To ask why?

To accept that you may
never know or be given

The answer,

trust faithful one, it's the only way

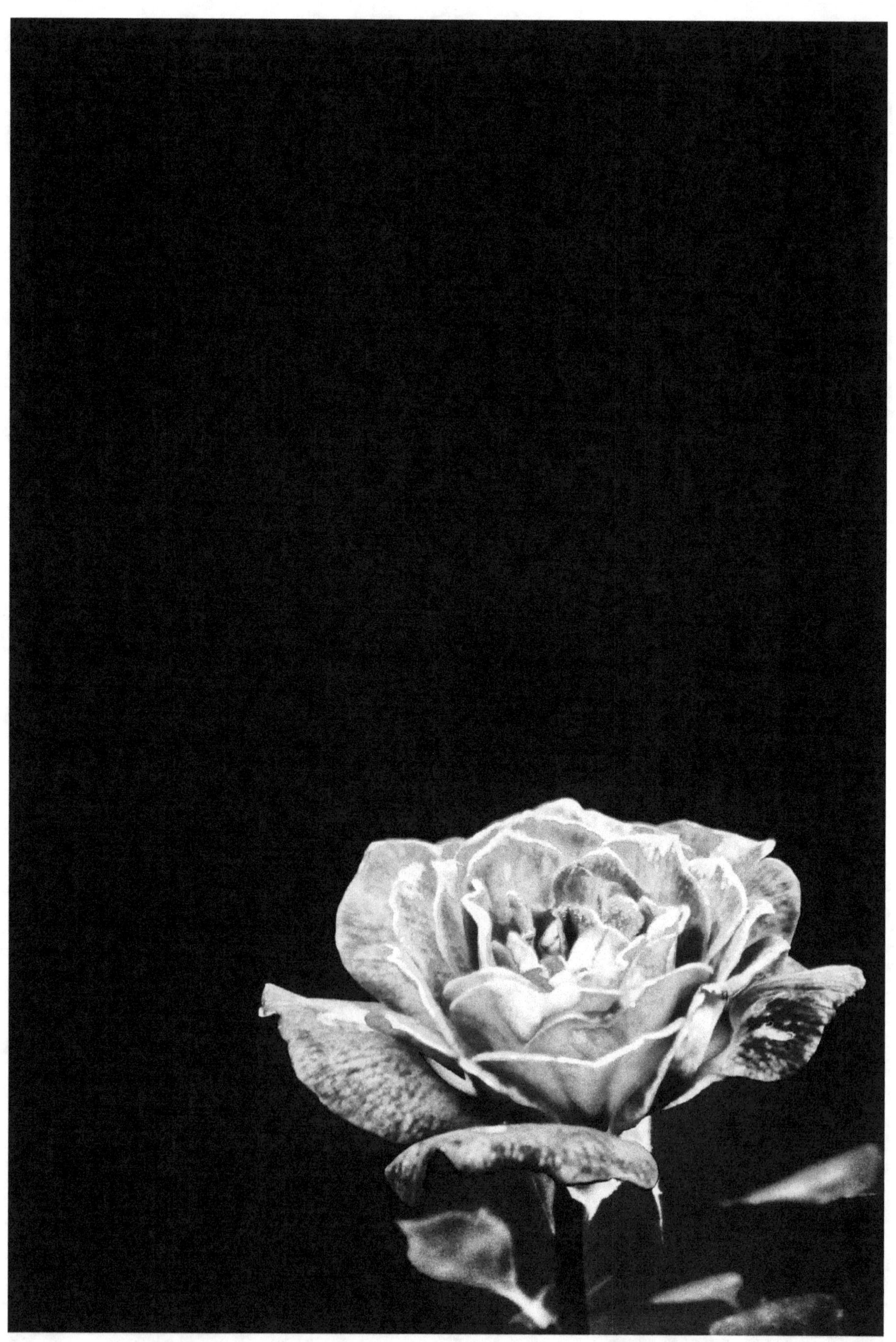

The People

Don't you hear it?
The uproar of the voices
How can we let those who only think of themselves rule?
Are we too busy to stop and listen?
The questions swirl around us
I believe the answer is also with the questions
What can it be?
Aren't we like them also?
We live in our own worlds
Hurrying from one hour to the next
Little ones are hurting, don't you know we are all little ones
Just because our bodies are older doesn't mean we don't cry
Or feed the inner needs
Truly one small thought or deed can change the world
Send a ripple that can't be stopped across the earth
Must believe there is hope
That every knee will bow down to the call

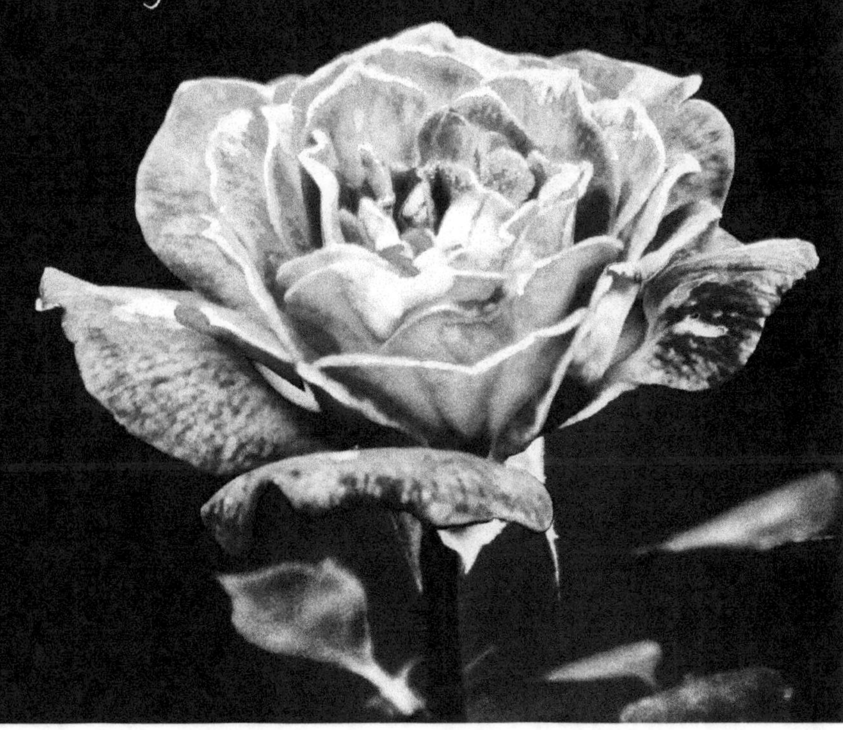

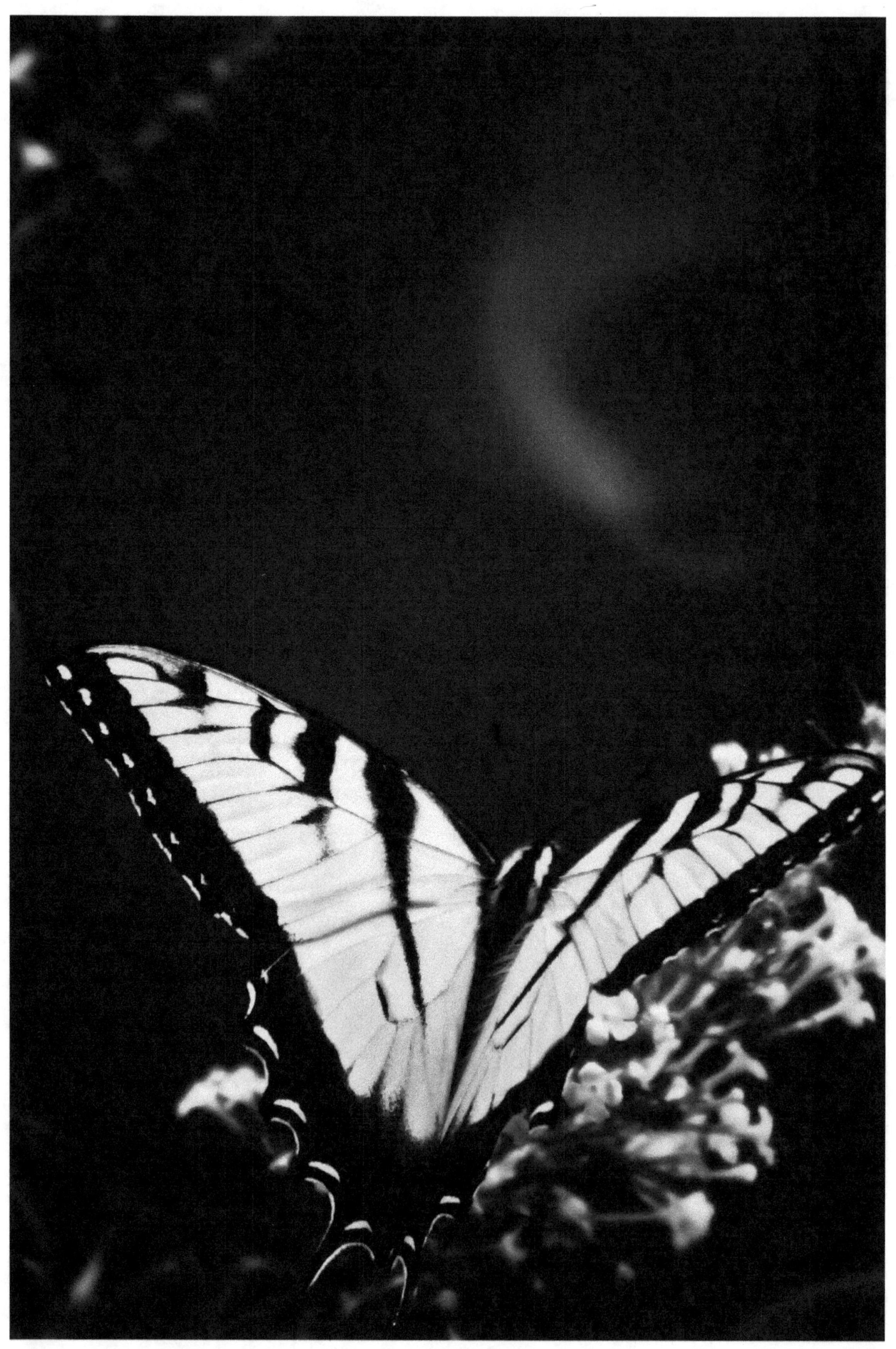

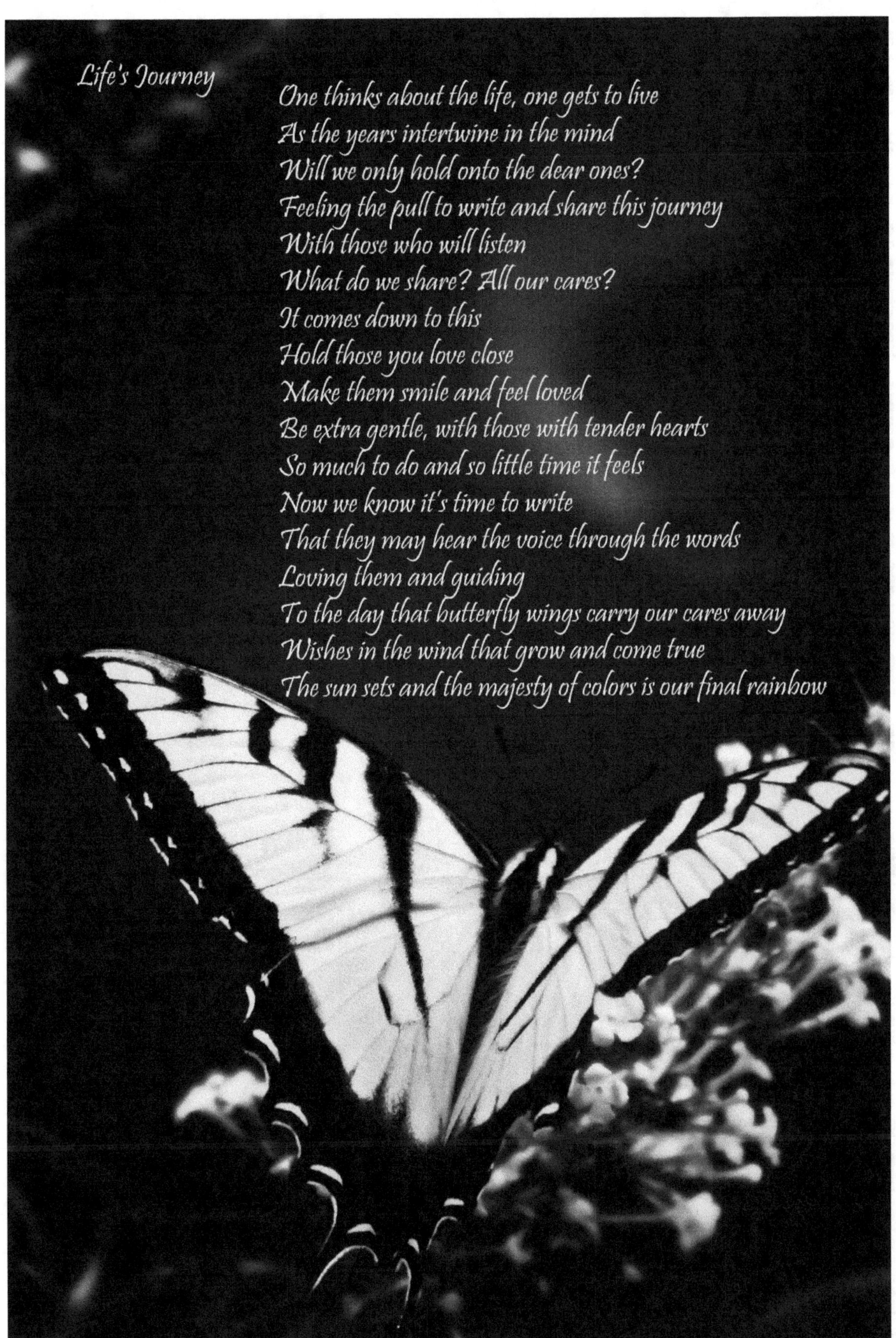
Life's Journey
One thinks about the life, one gets to live
As the years intertwine in the mind
Will we only hold onto the dear ones?
Feeling the pull to write and share this journey
With those who will listen
What do we share? All our cares?
It comes down to this
Hold those you love close
Make them smile and feel loved
Be extra gentle, with those with tender hearts
So much to do and so little time it feels
Now we know it's time to write
That they may hear the voice through the words
Loving them and guiding
To the day that butterfly wings carry our cares away
Wishes in the wind that grow and come true
The sun sets and the majesty of colors is our final rainbow

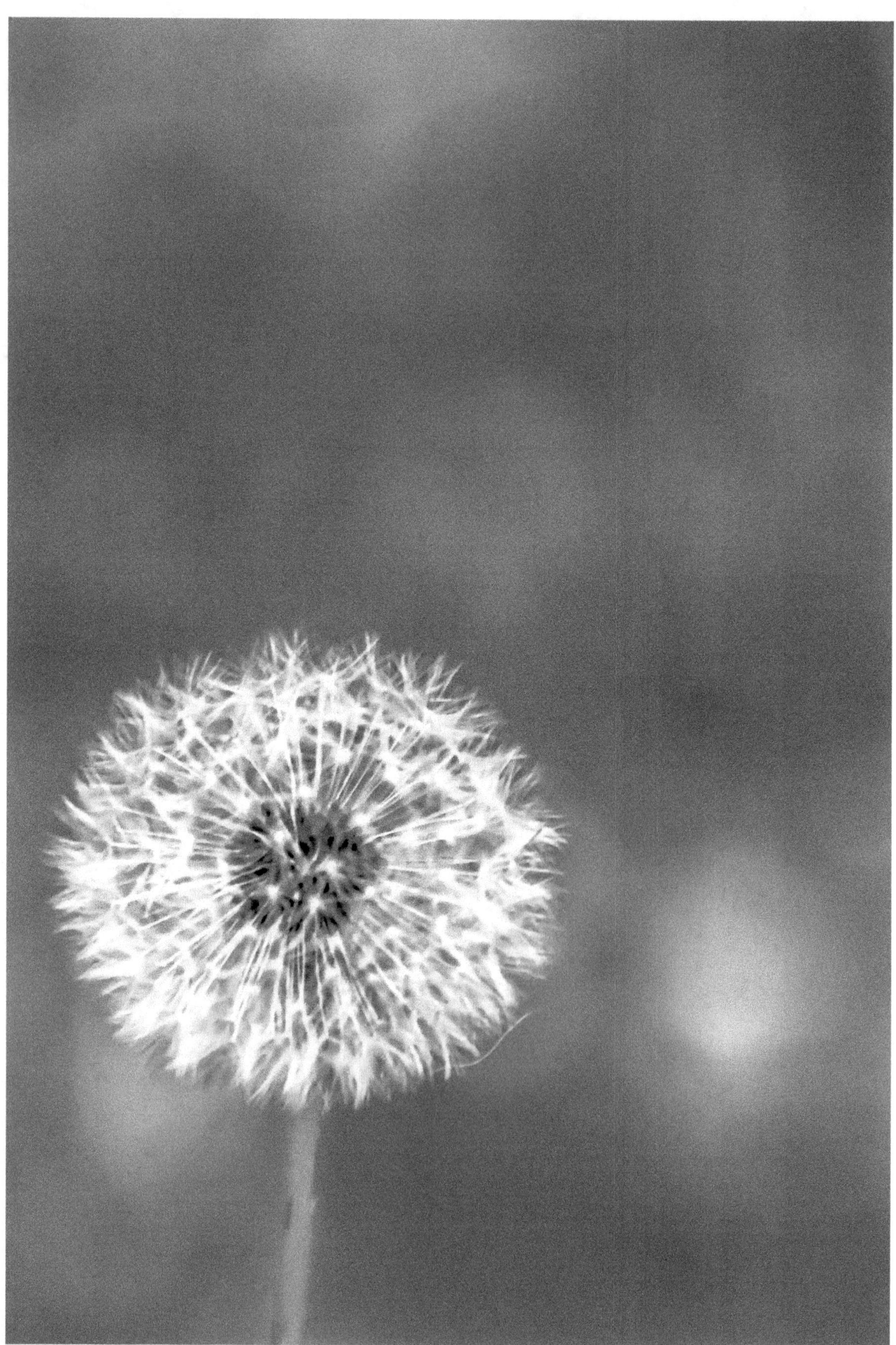

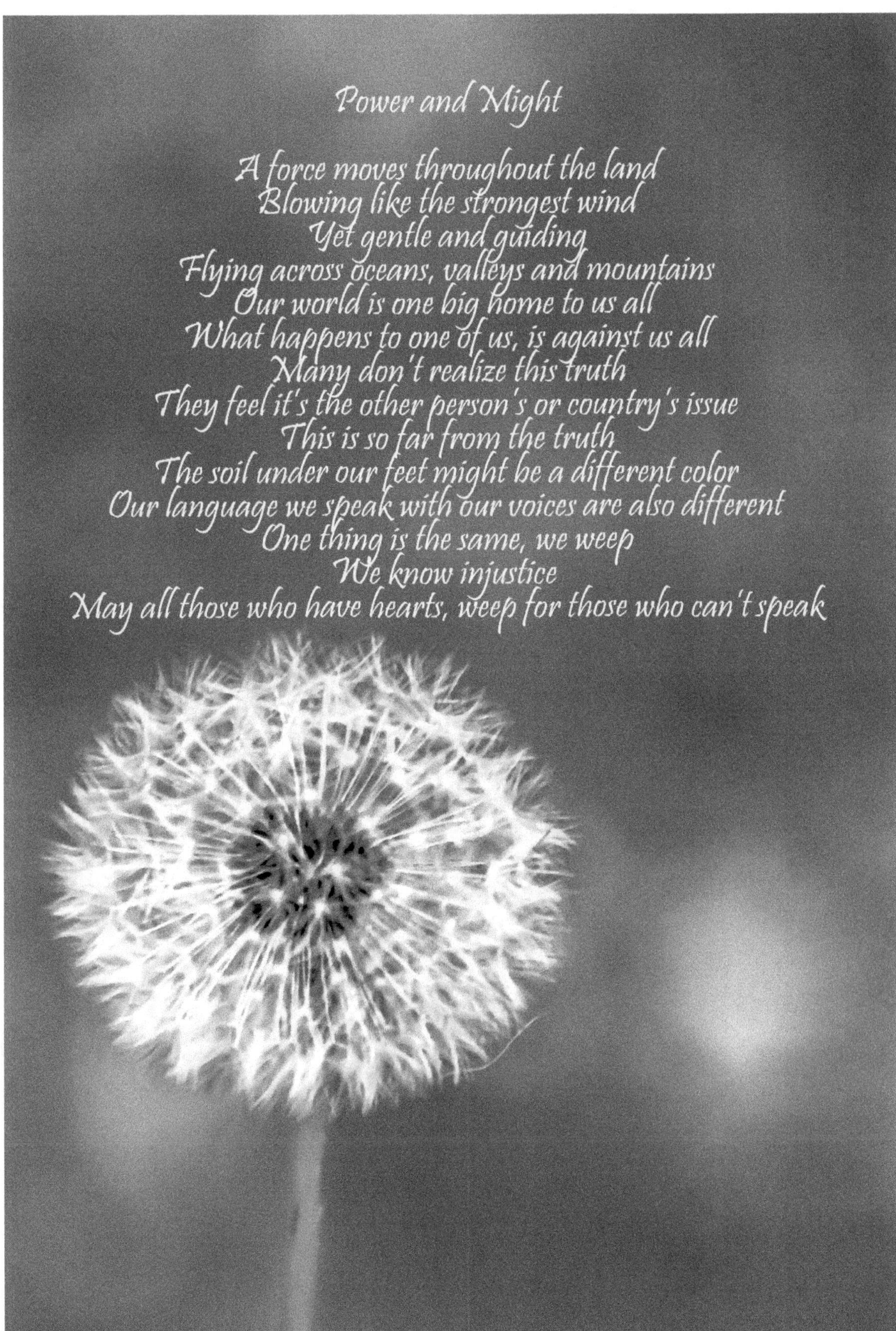
Power and Might
A force moves throughout the land
Blowing like the strongest wind
Yet gentle and guiding
Flying across oceans, valleys and mountains
Our world is one big home to us all
What happens to one of us, is against us all
Many don't realize this truth
They feel it's the other person's or country's issue
This is so far from the truth
The soil under our feet might be a different color
Our language we speak with our voices are also different
One thing is the same, we weep
We know injustice
May all those who have hearts, weep for those who can't speak

Alone Warrior

Pain is deep
More than anyone can imagine
The real warriors are hidden until their time has come to be revealed
They are bruised and have had their hearts broken
This is how they can stand when everyone around them falls
It comes from a well inside them that is always flowing
Carrying on is the only option
I have witnessed this first hand
When truth is placed in one's heart you can't stand untruth
Love surrounds and protects those who ask
Gentle and folding around like soft petals
This is what the alone warrior learns, they are never alone
Guided by heavenly hosts, whispering hymns and praise
Golden is the face that reflects the sun
Wings are given, take flight my warrior

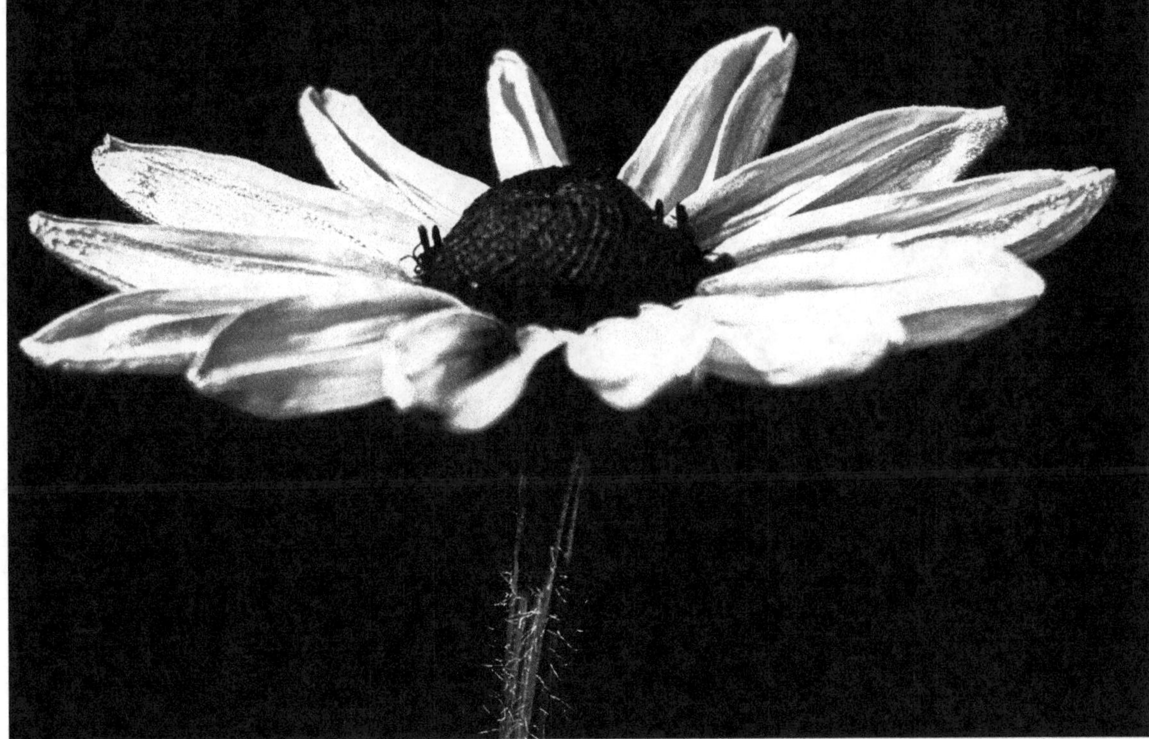

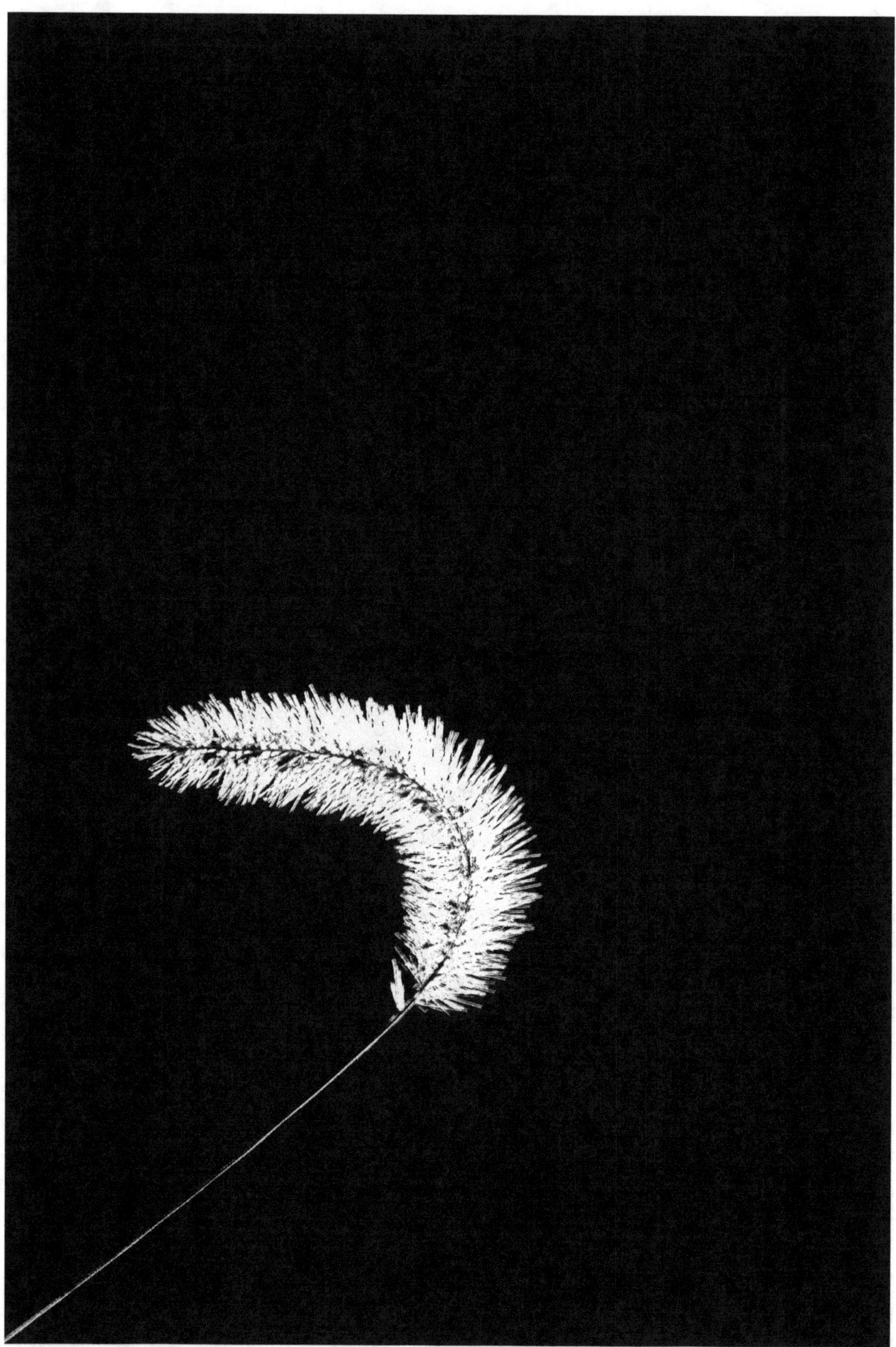

The Answer

Confession begins
In my artless simplicity, here I am
I know whom I have believed
How unspeakably blessed such realization is!
Not universal or even common
One's heart is in line with the truths
When others do not care to see or hear the cries
How does one stand up in an ocean so deep?
I know there is an island for those who seek
And want to whisper scream please stop
If we take life from our little ones what is left?
The answers lay in the broken hearts
From ashes comes the hope
Like a brilliant star in the darkest night

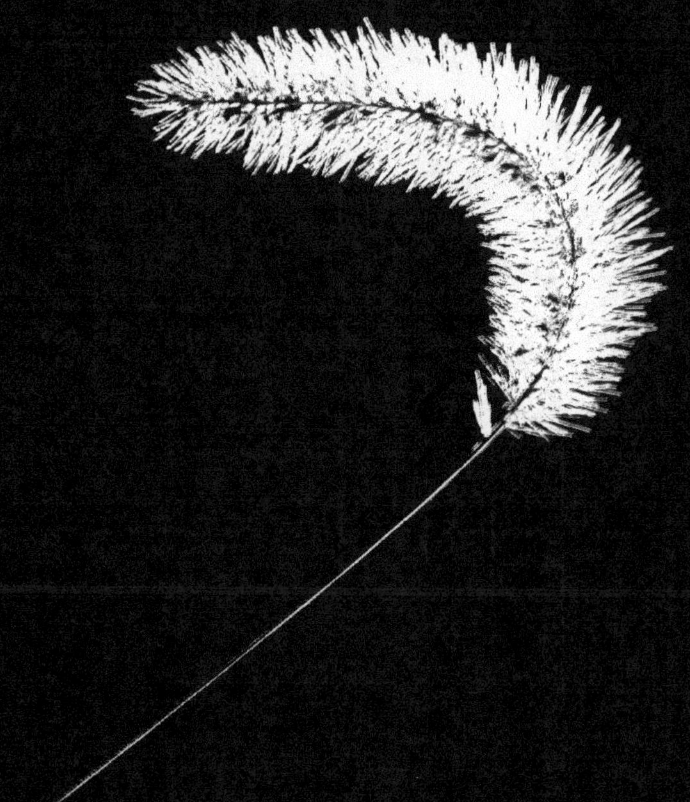

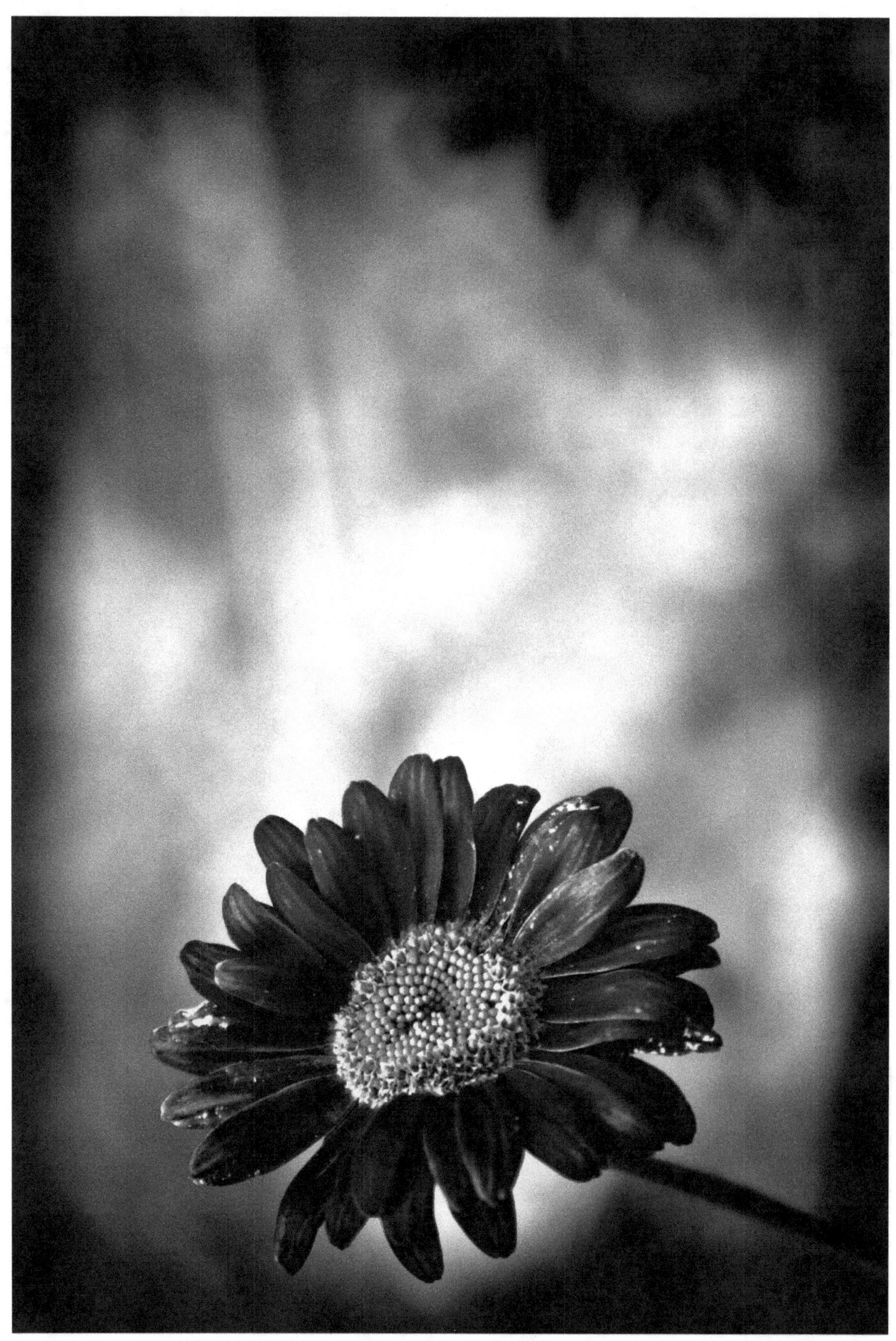

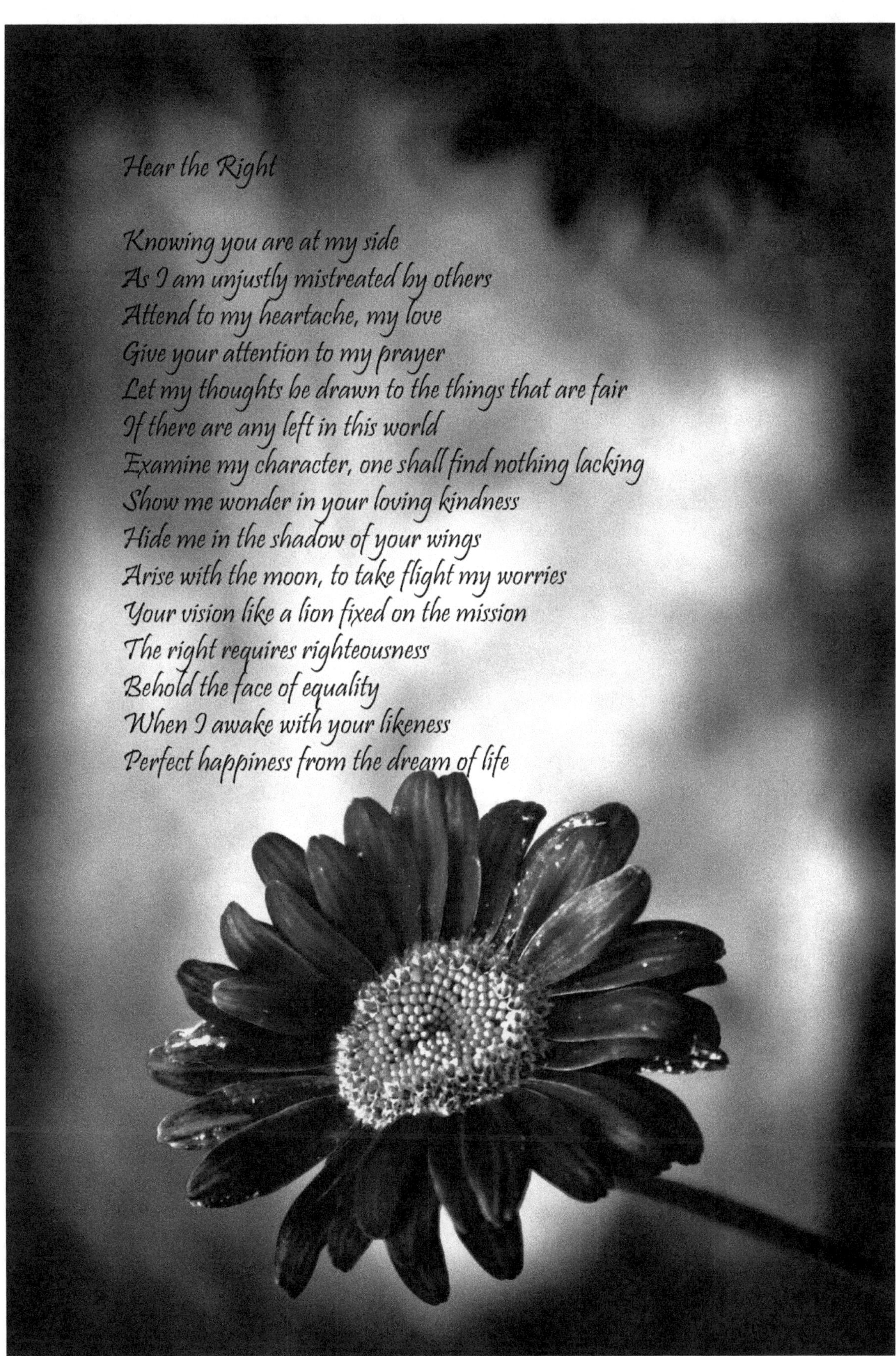

Hear the Right

Knowing you are at my side
As I am unjustly mistreated by others
Attend to my heartache, my love
Give your attention to my prayer
Let my thoughts be drawn to the things that are fair
If there are any left in this world
Examine my character, one shall find nothing lacking
Show me wonder in your loving kindness
Hide me in the shadow of your wings
Arise with the moon, to take flight my worries
Your vision like a lion fixed on the mission
The right requires righteousness
Behold the face of equality
When I awake with your likeness
Perfect happiness from the dream of life

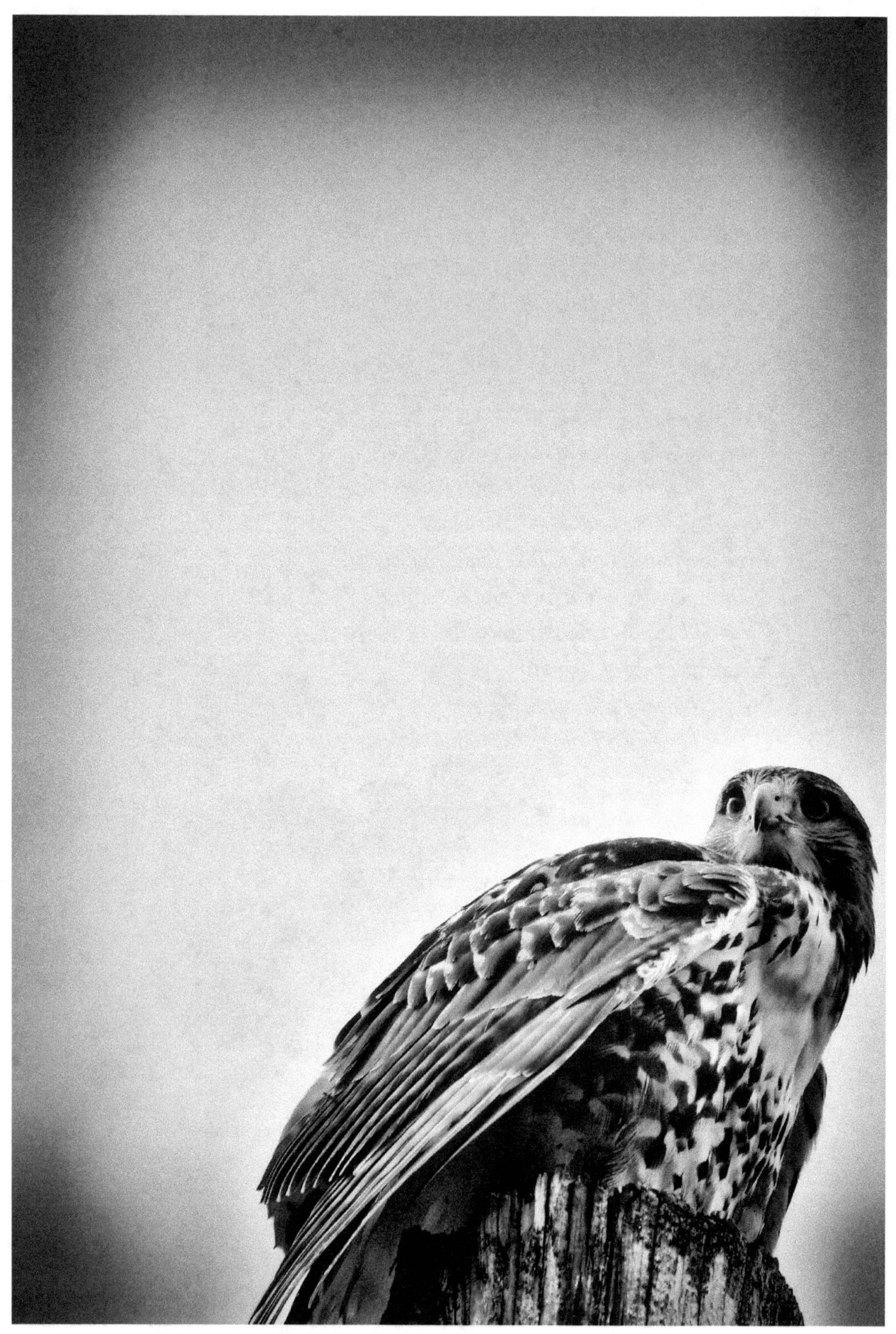

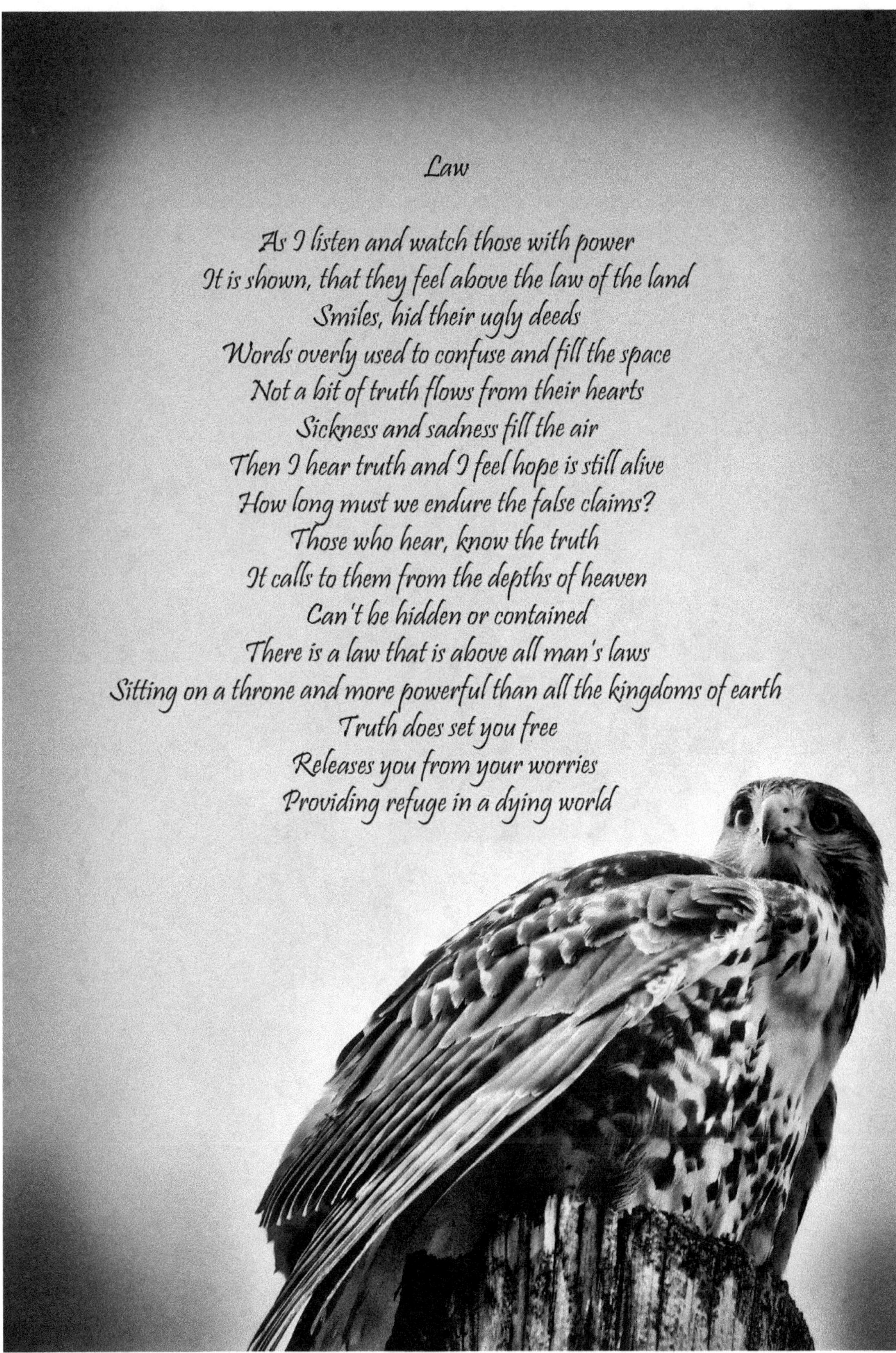

Law

As I listen and watch those with power
It is shown, that they feel above the law of the land
Smiles, hid their ugly deeds
Words overly used to confuse and fill the space
Not a bit of truth flows from their hearts
Sickness and sadness fill the air
Then I hear truth and I feel hope is still alive
How long must we endure the false claims?
Those who hear, know the truth
It calls to them from the depths of heaven
Can't be hidden or contained
There is a law that is above all man's laws
Sitting on a throne and more powerful than all the kingdoms of earth
Truth does set you free
Releases you from your worries
Providing refuge in a dying world

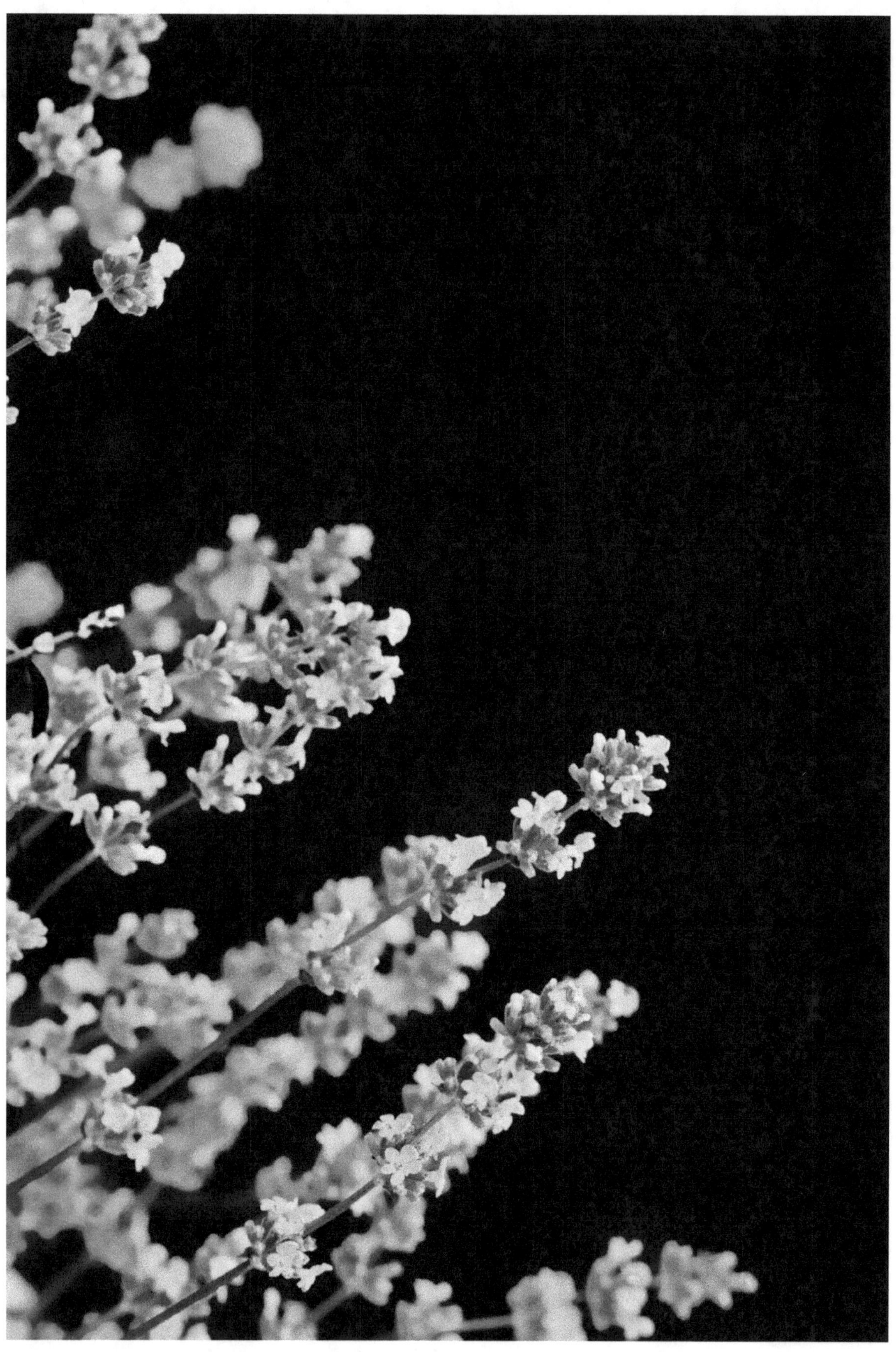

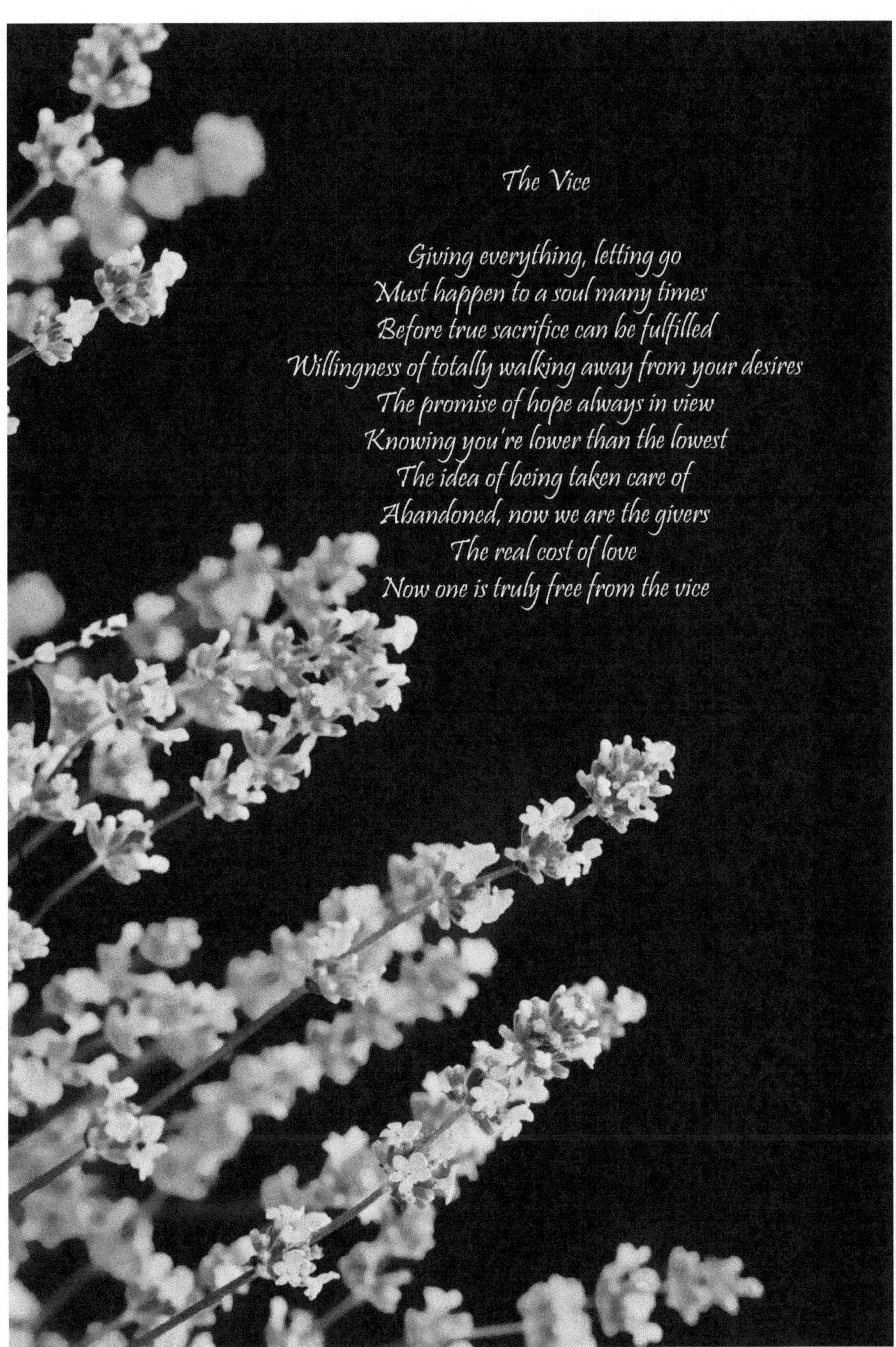

The Vice

Giving everything, letting go
Must happen to a soul many times
Before true sacrifice can be fulfilled
Willingness of totally walking away from your desires
The promise of hope always in view
Knowing you're lower than the lowest
The idea of being taken care of
Abandoned, now we are the givers
The real cost of love
Now one is truly free from the vice

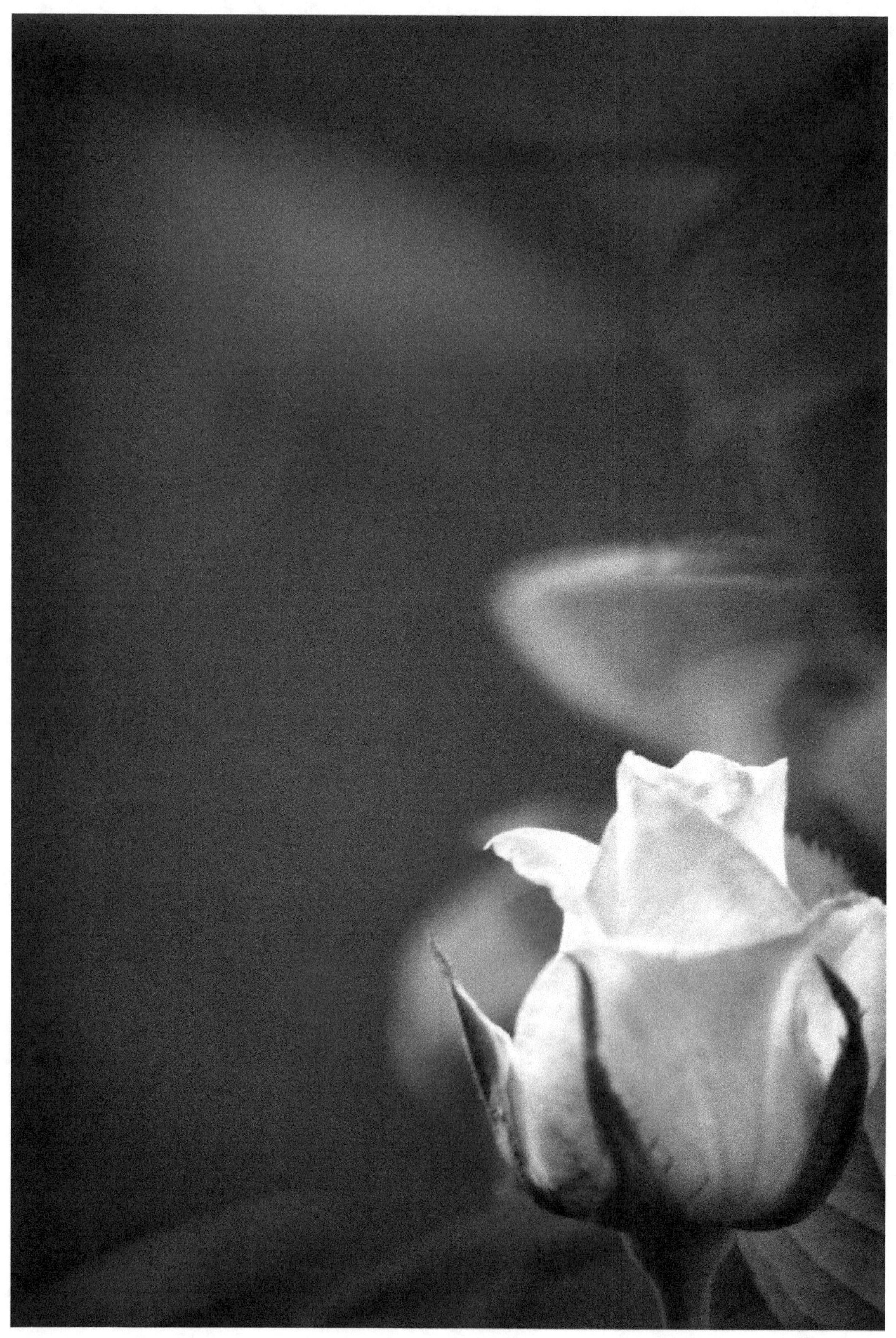

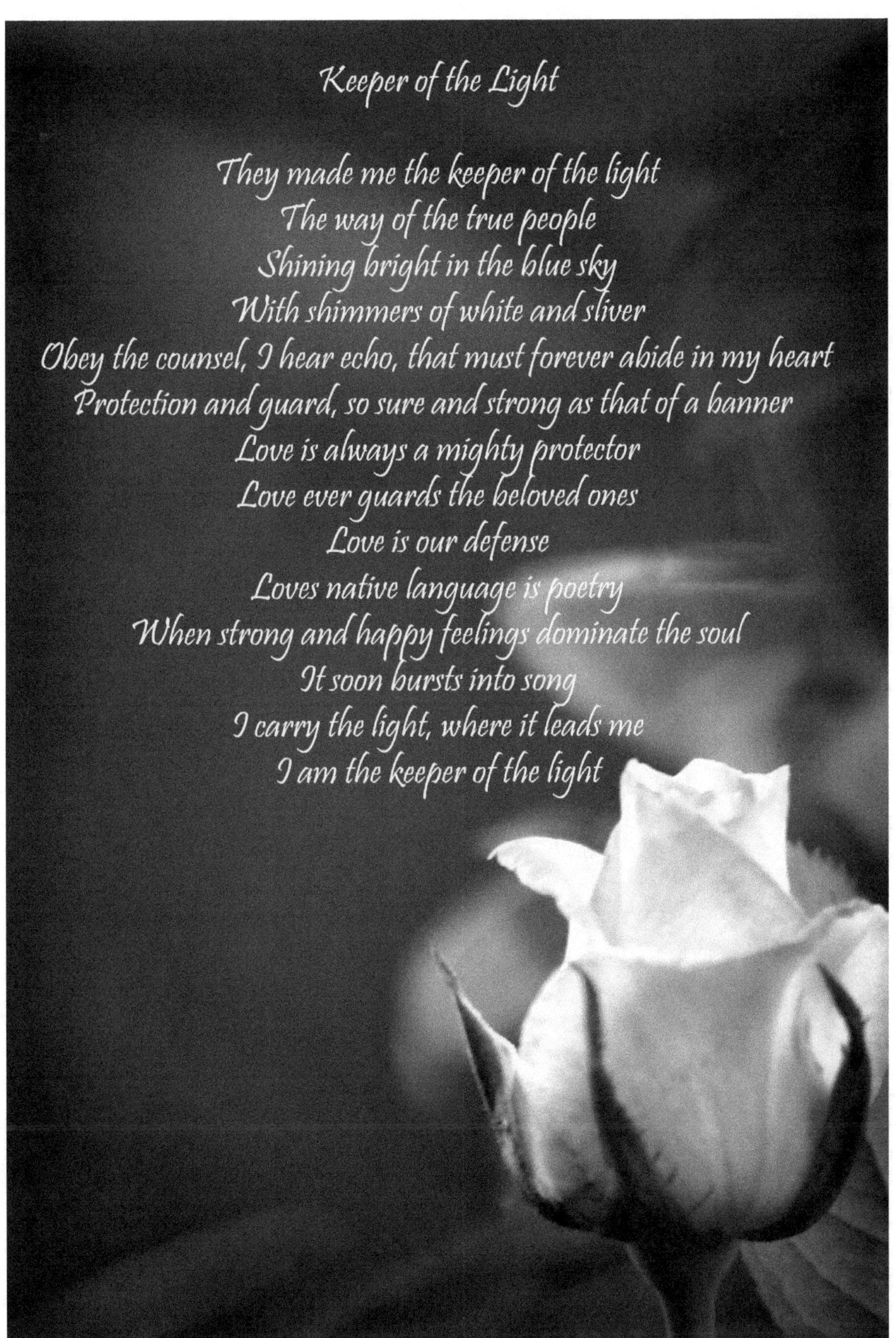
Keeper of the Light
They made me the keeper of the light
The way of the true people
Shining bright in the blue sky
With shimmers of white and sliver
Obey the counsel, I hear echo, that must forever abide in my heart
Protection and guard, so sure and strong as that of a banner
Love is always a mighty protector
Love ever guards the beloved ones
Love is our defense
Loves native language is poetry
When strong and happy feelings dominate the soul
It soon bursts into song
I carry the light, where it leads me
I am the keeper of the light

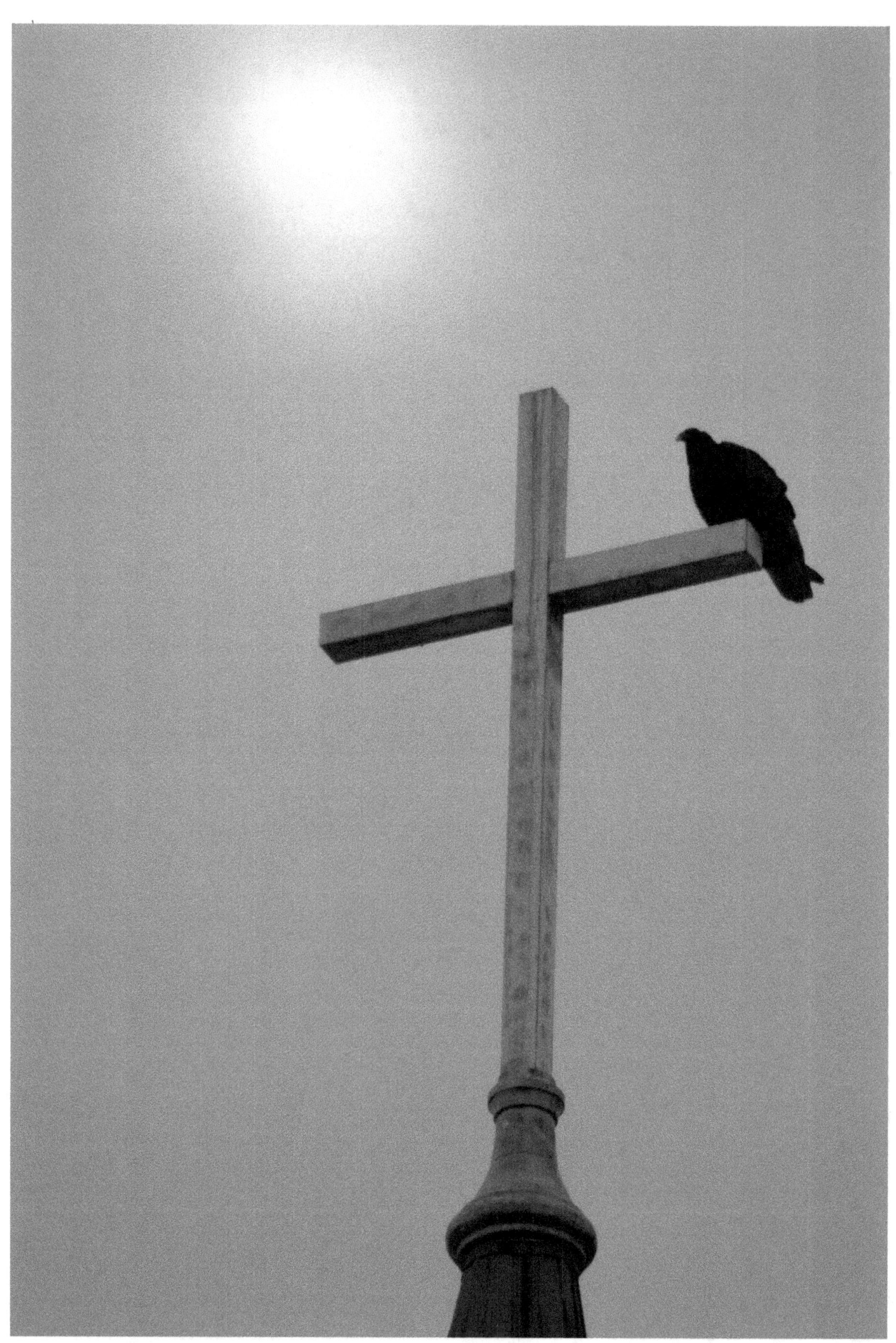

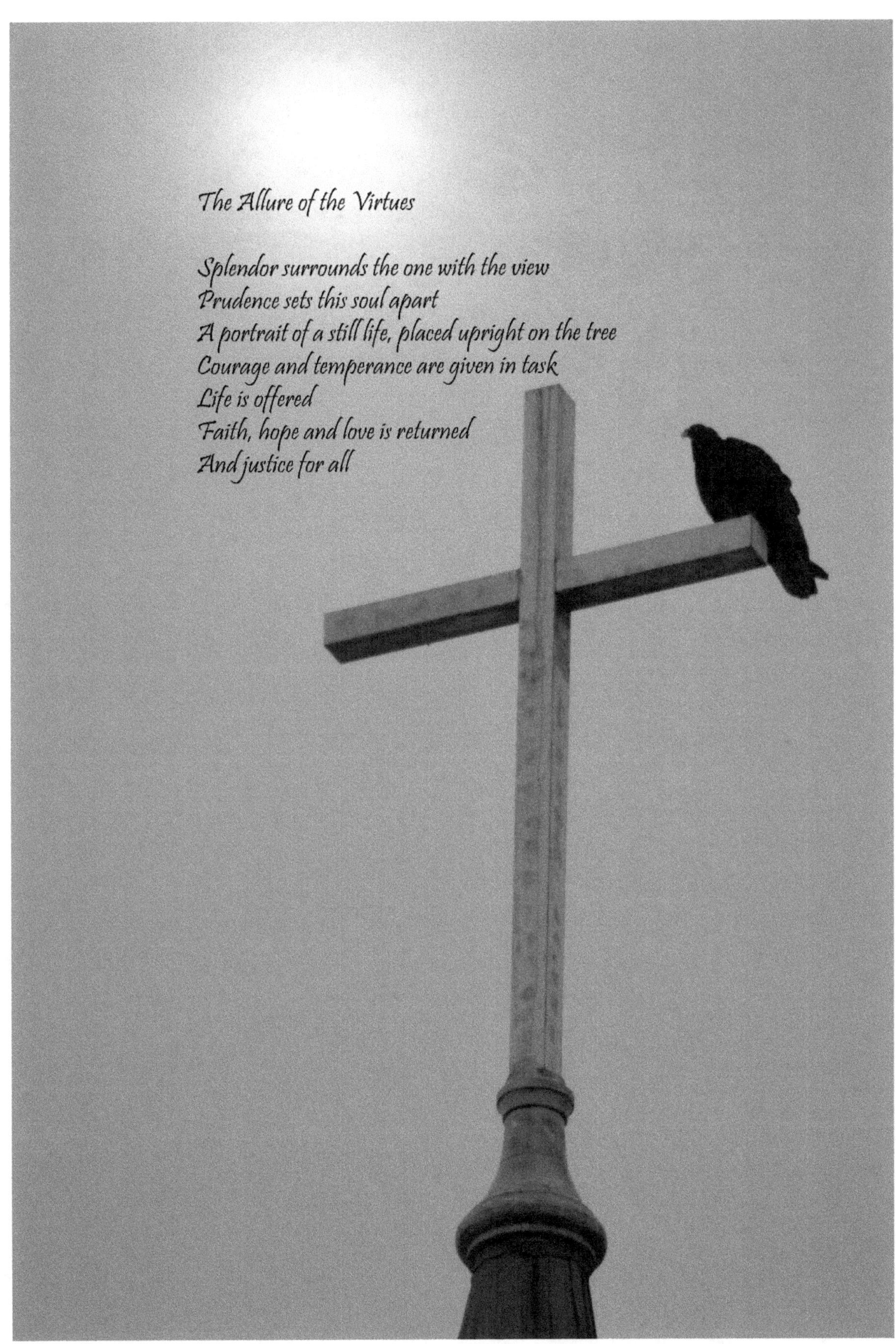

The Allure of the Virtues

Splendor surrounds the one with the view
Prudence sets this soul apart
A portrait of a still life, placed upright on the tree
Courage and temperance are given in task
Life is offered
Faith, hope and love is returned
And justice for all

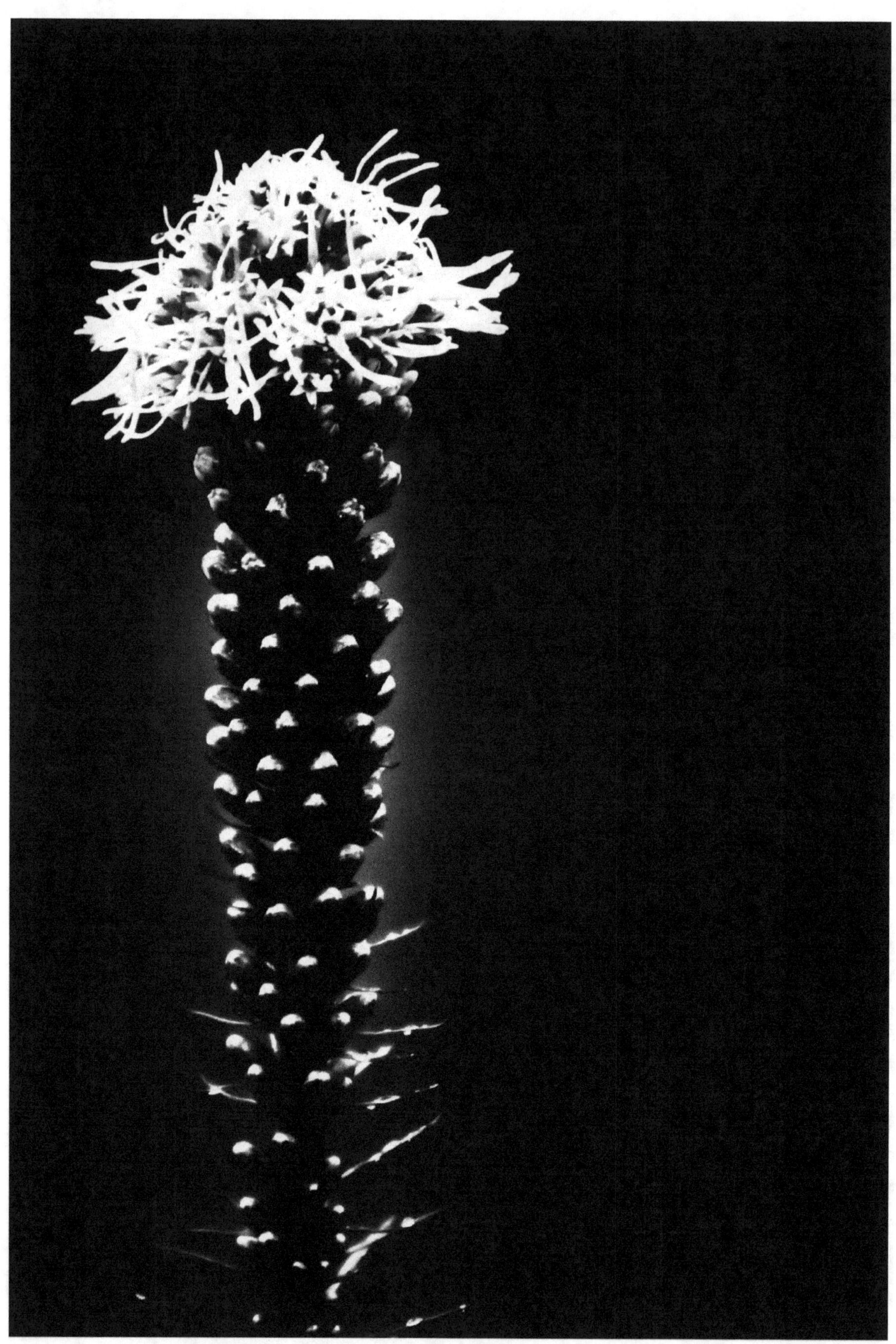

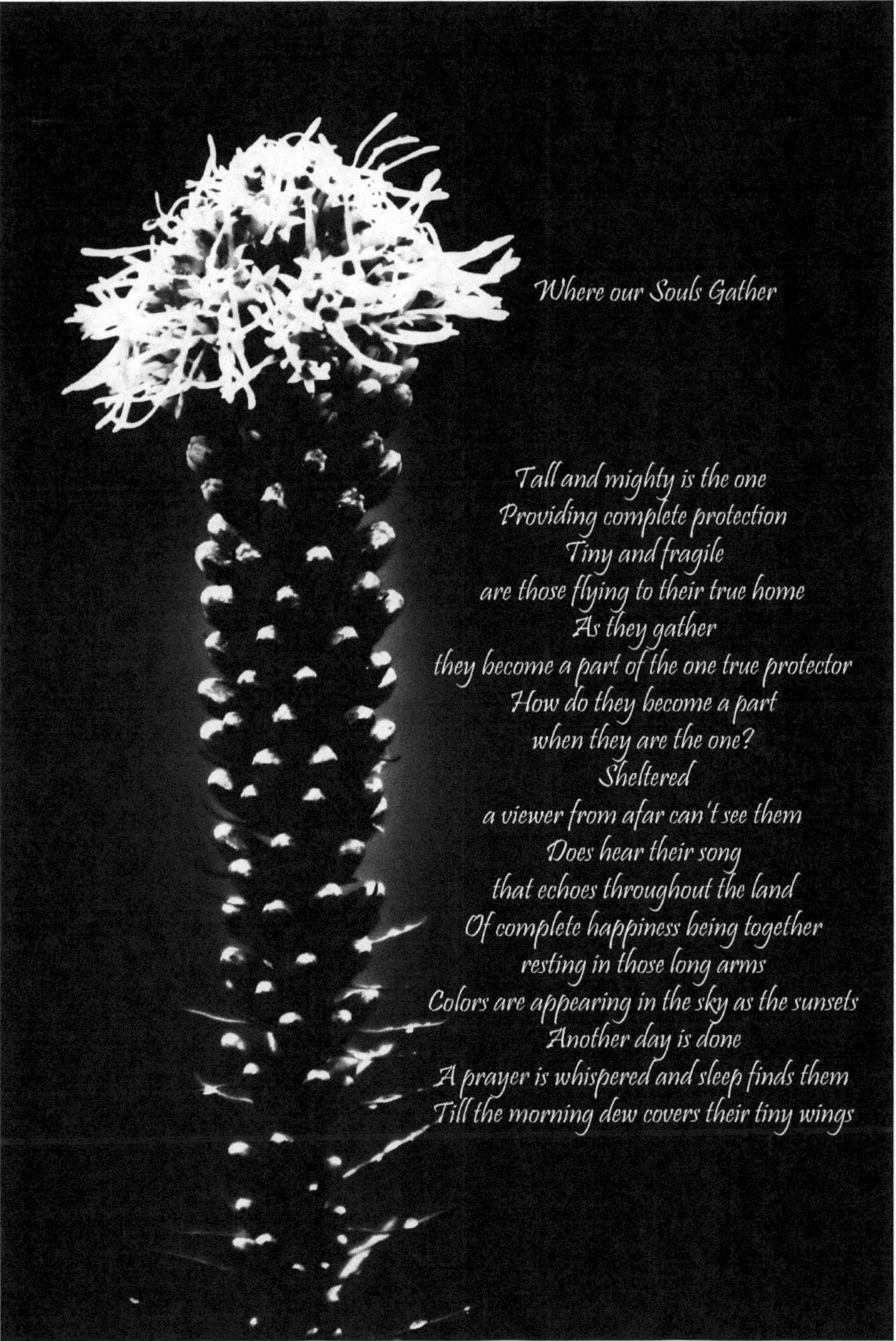
Where our Souls Gather
Tall and mighty is the one
Providing complete protection
Tiny and fragile
are those flying to their true home
As they gather
they become a part of the one true protector
How do they become a part
when they are the one?
Sheltered
a viewer from afar can't see them
Does hear their song
that echoes throughout the land
Of complete happiness being together
resting in those long arms
Colors are appearing in the sky as the sunsets
Another day is done
A prayer is whispered and sleep finds them
Till the morning dew covers their tiny wings

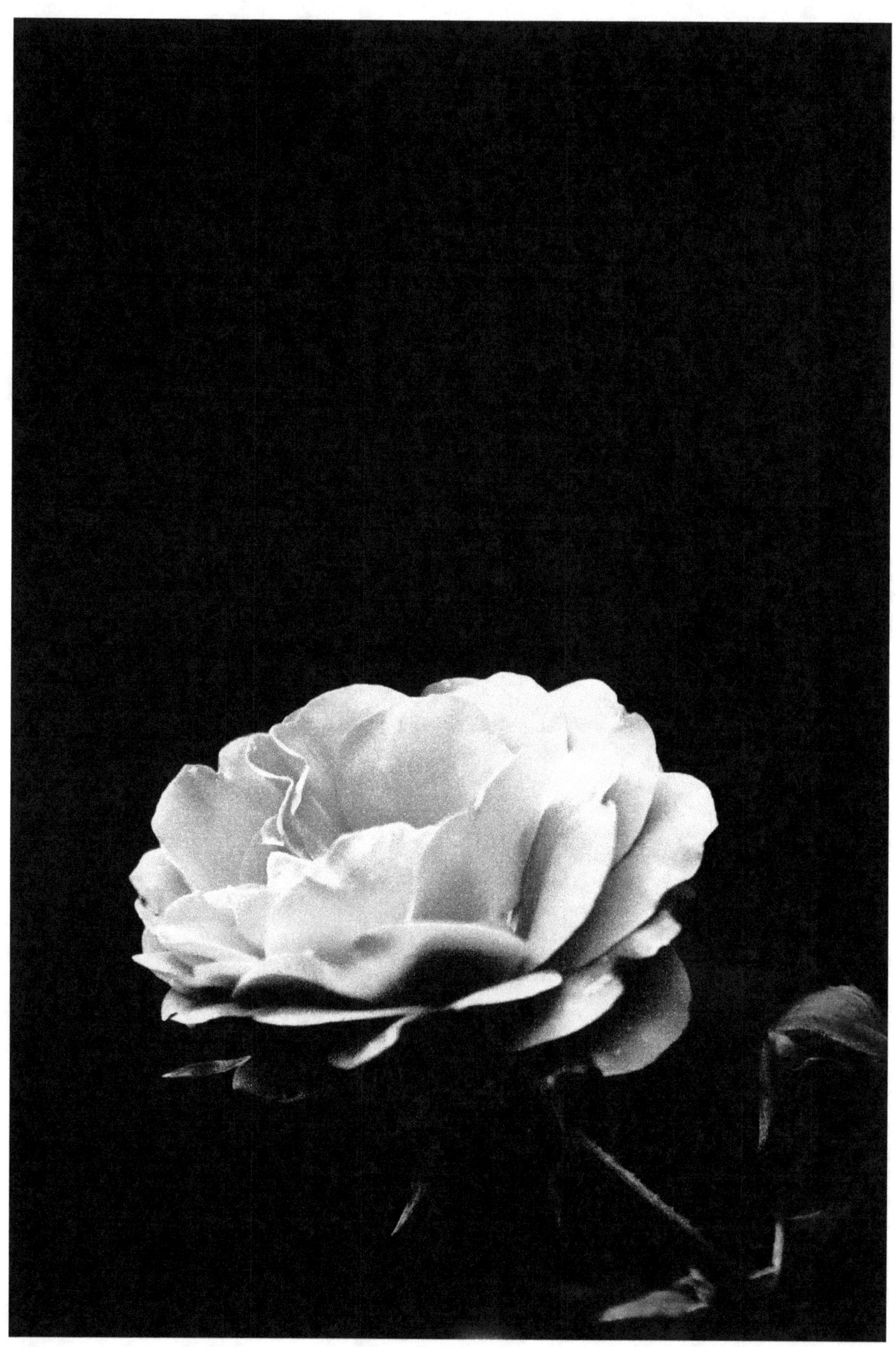

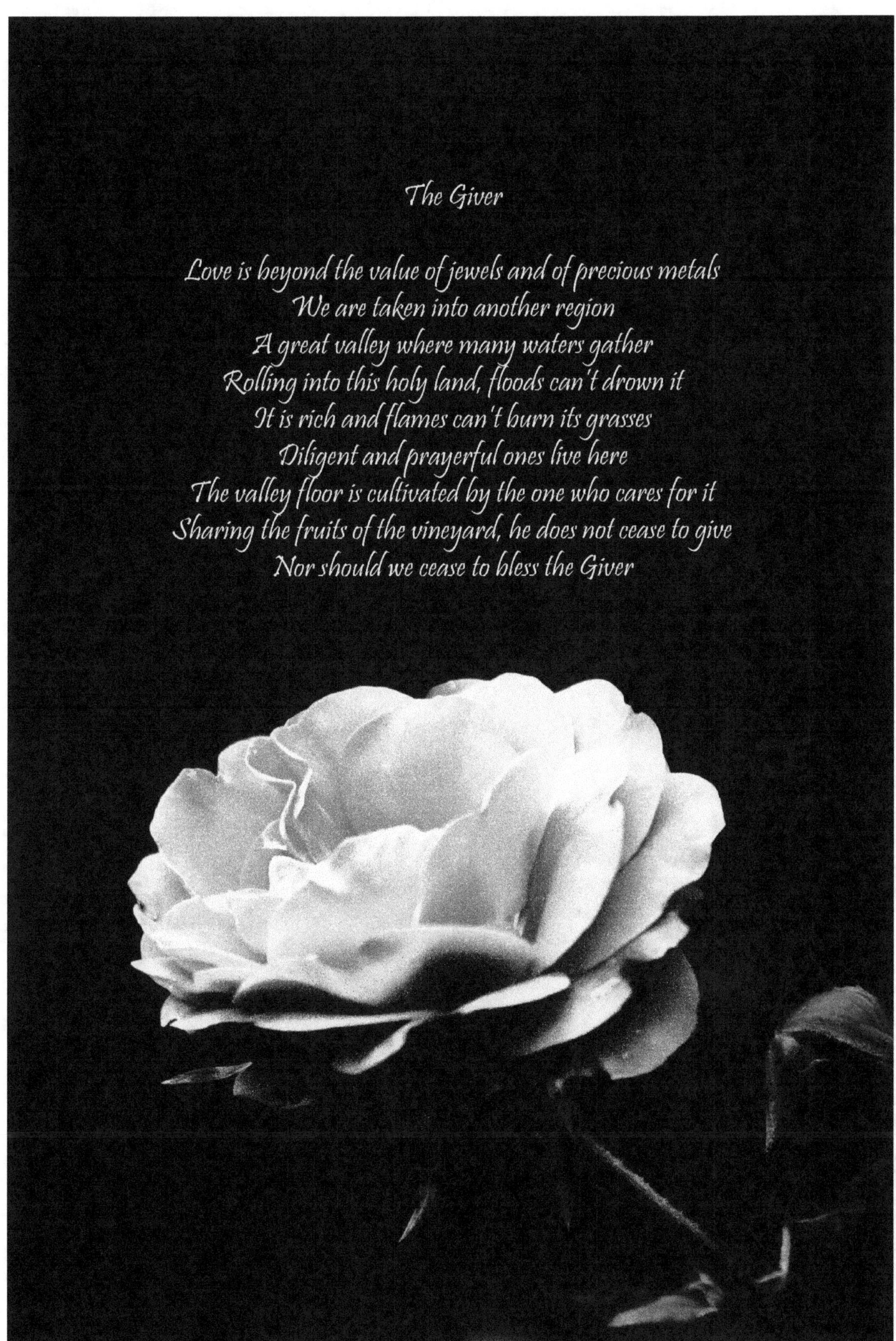

The Giver

Love is beyond the value of jewels and of precious metals
We are taken into another region
A great valley where many waters gather
Rolling into this holy land, floods can't drown it
It is rich and flames can't burn its grasses
Diligent and prayerful ones live here
The valley floor is cultivated by the one who cares for it
Sharing the fruits of the vineyard, he does not cease to give
Nor should we cease to bless the Giver

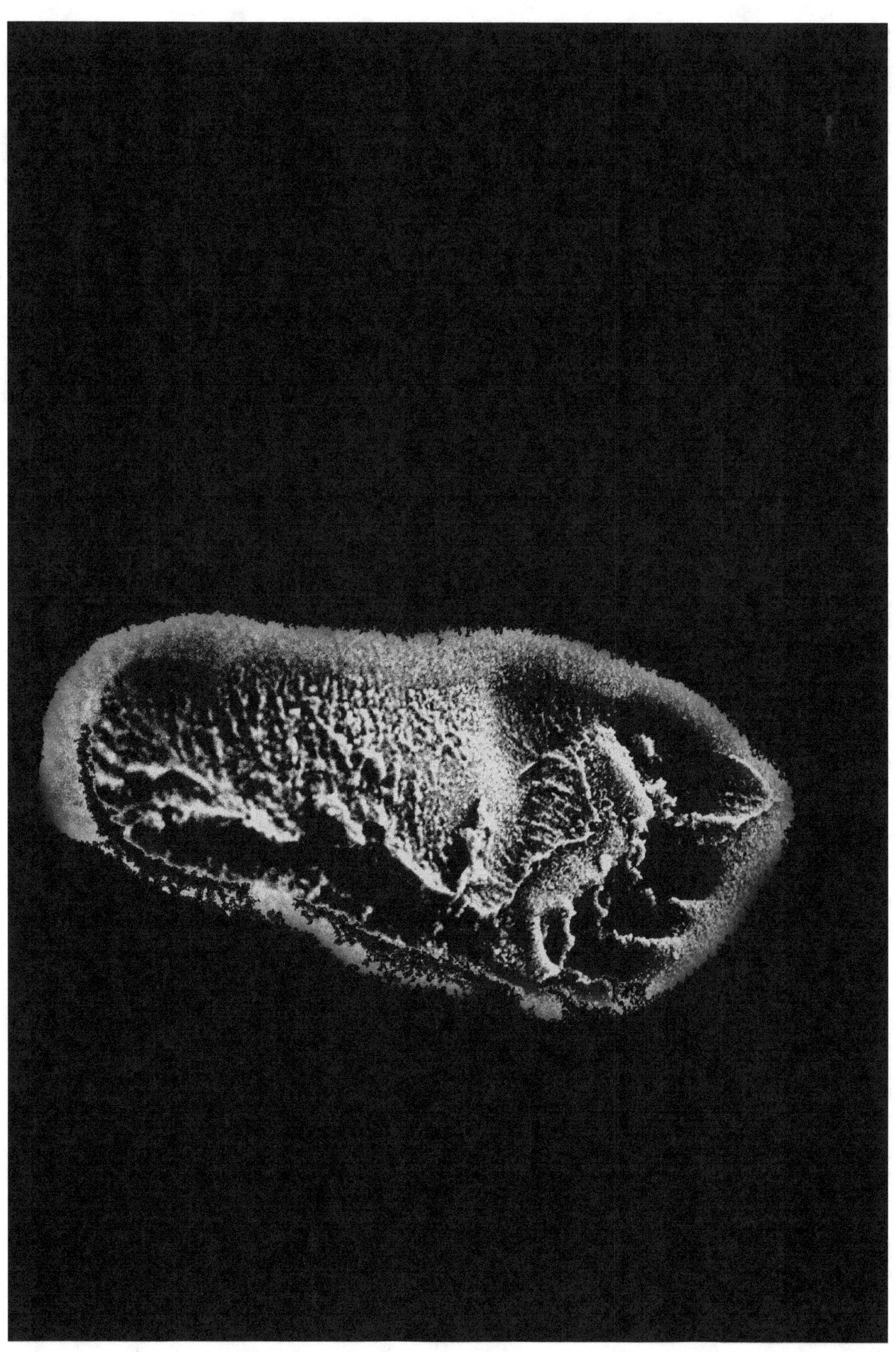

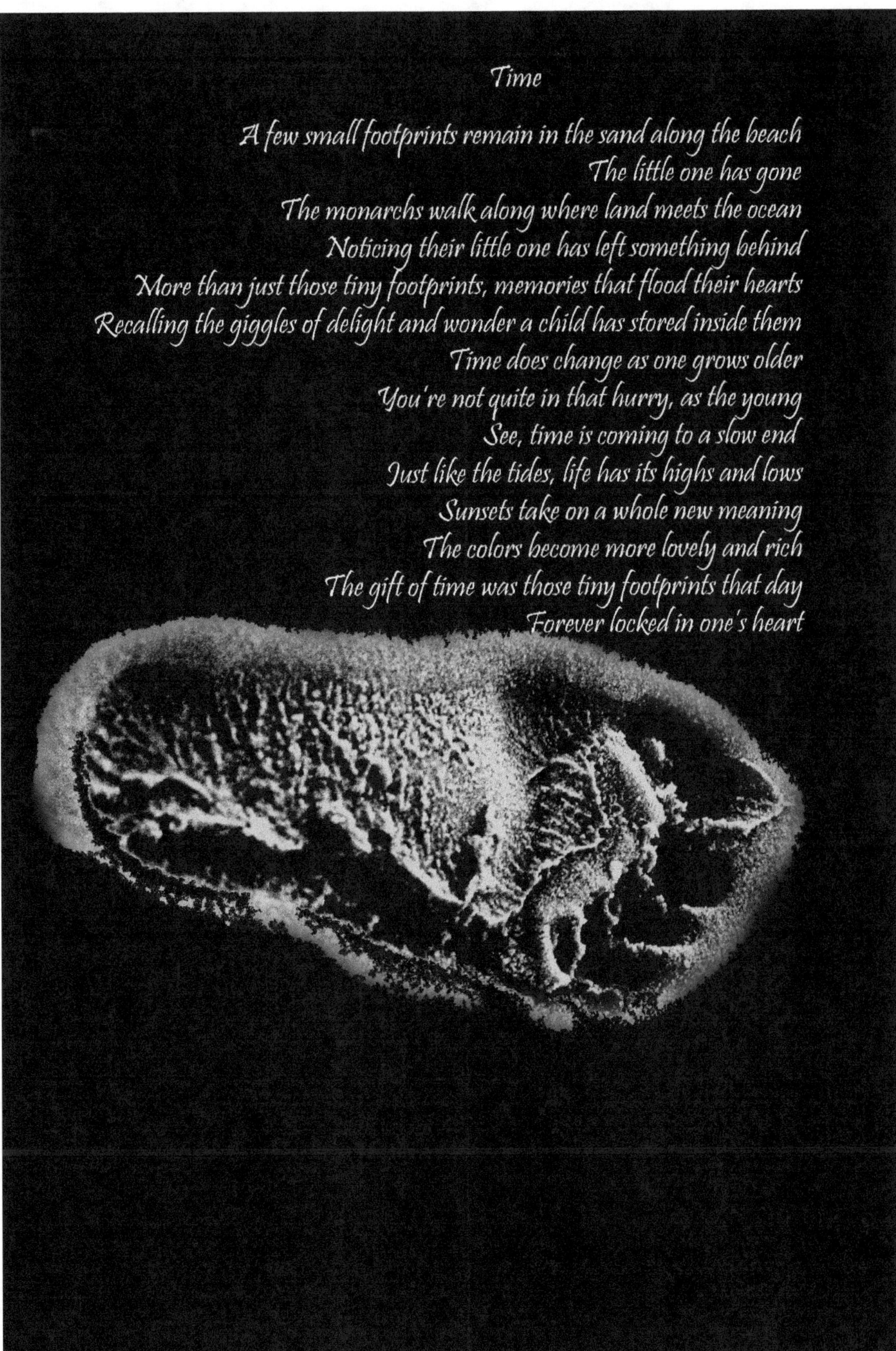

Time

A few small footprints remain in the sand along the beach
The little one has gone
The monarchs walk along where land meets the ocean
Noticing their little one has left something behind
More than just those tiny footprints, memories that flood their hearts
Recalling the giggles of delight and wonder a child has stored inside them
Time does change as one grows older
You're not quite in that hurry, as the young
See, time is coming to a slow end
Just like the tides, life has its highs and lows
Sunsets take on a whole new meaning
The colors become more lovely and rich
The gift of time was those tiny footprints that day
Forever locked in one's heart

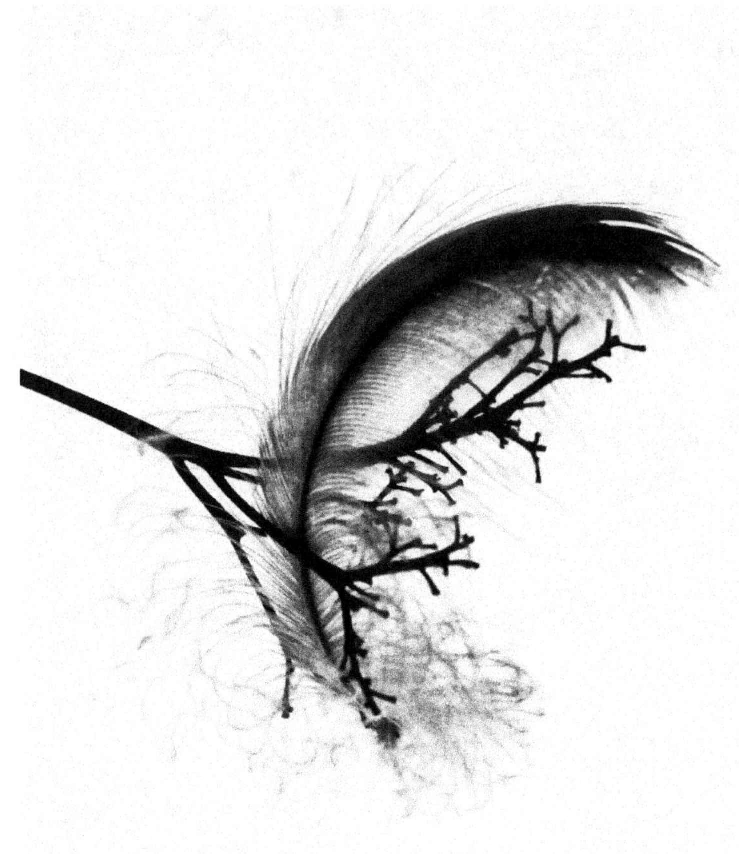

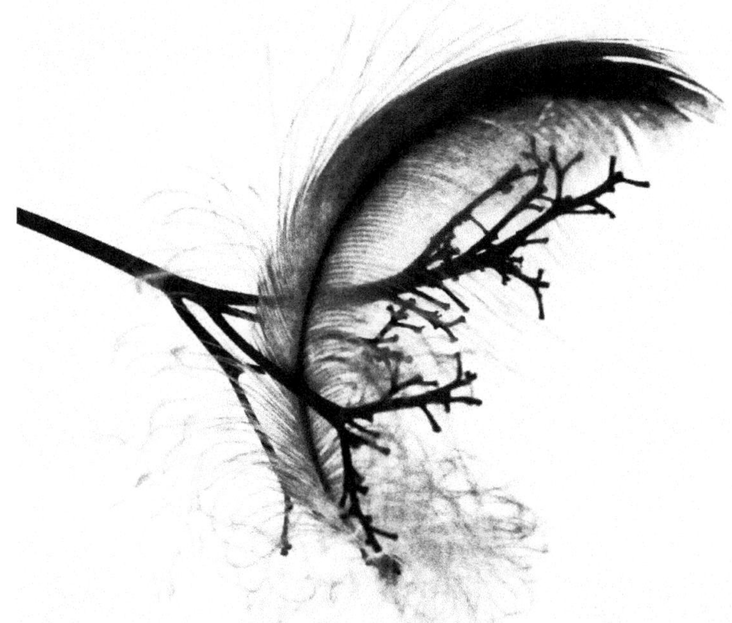

The Feather of Hope

Sitting alongside a small brook
A white feather floated in the air from above
Divine communion we shared that day
The agency of Angels giving us the sign
One was close, protecting us from harm and giving hope
War, illness and time was showing on our hearts
We were reminded
How we are the very jewels in the crown
Listening to the sounds of nature
Basking in the light of light
The feather of hope was given in a vision before us

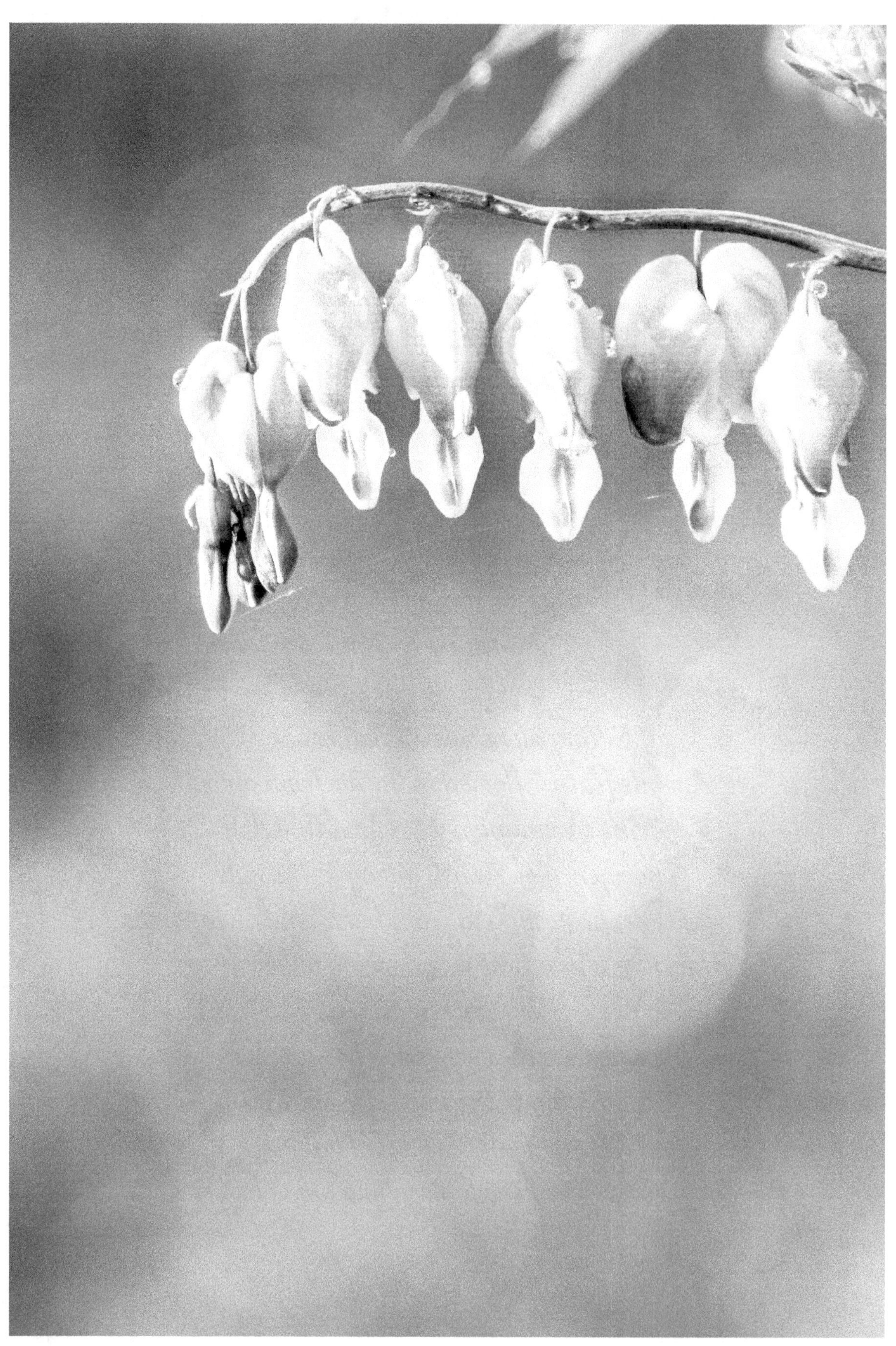

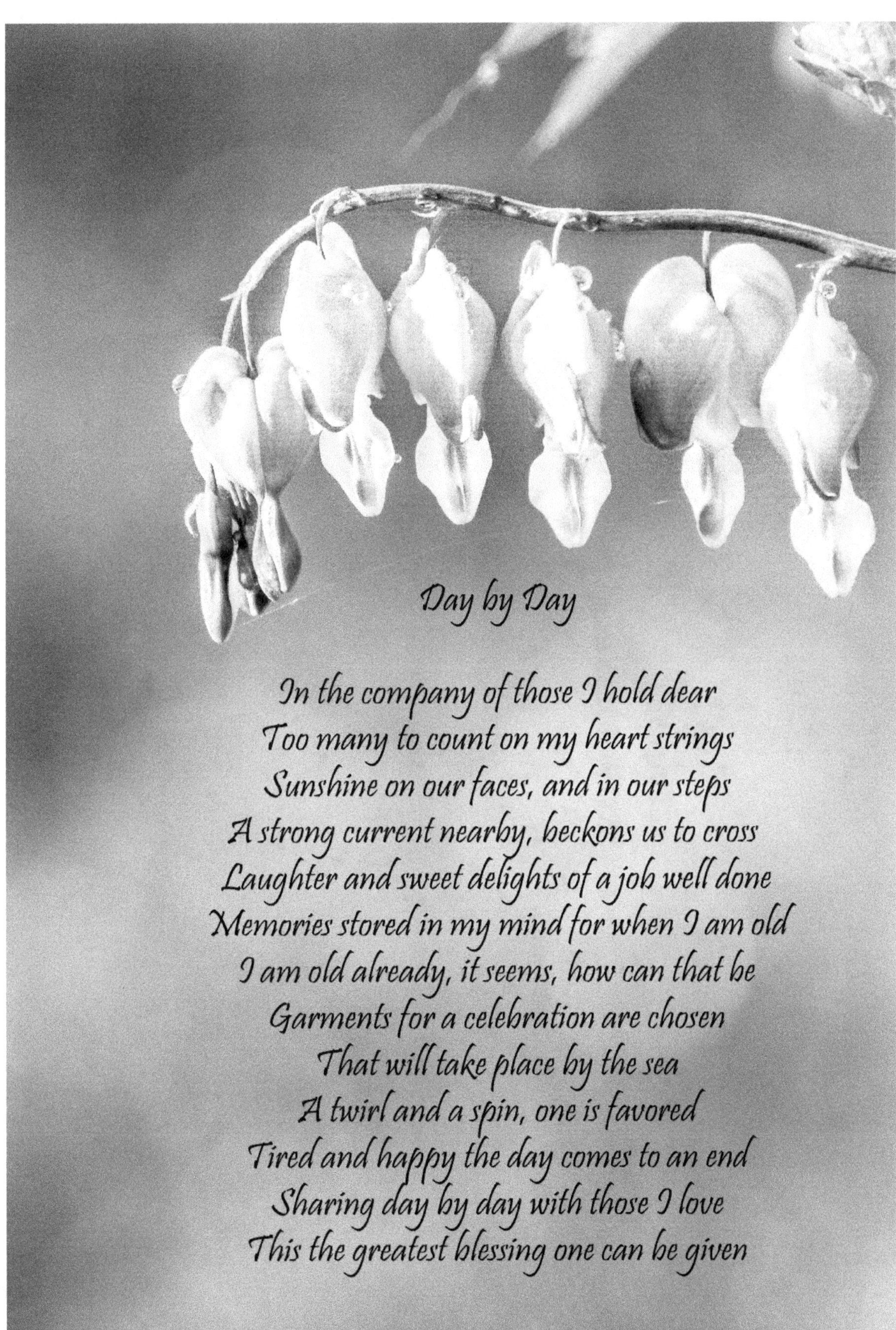

Day by Day

In the company of those I hold dear
Too many to count on my heart strings
Sunshine on our faces, and in our steps
A strong current nearby, beckons us to cross
Laughter and sweet delights of a job well done
Memories stored in my mind for when I am old
I am old already, it seems, how can that be
Garments for a celebration are chosen
That will take place by the sea
A twirl and a spin, one is favored
Tired and happy the day comes to an end
Sharing day by day with those I love
This the greatest blessing one can be given

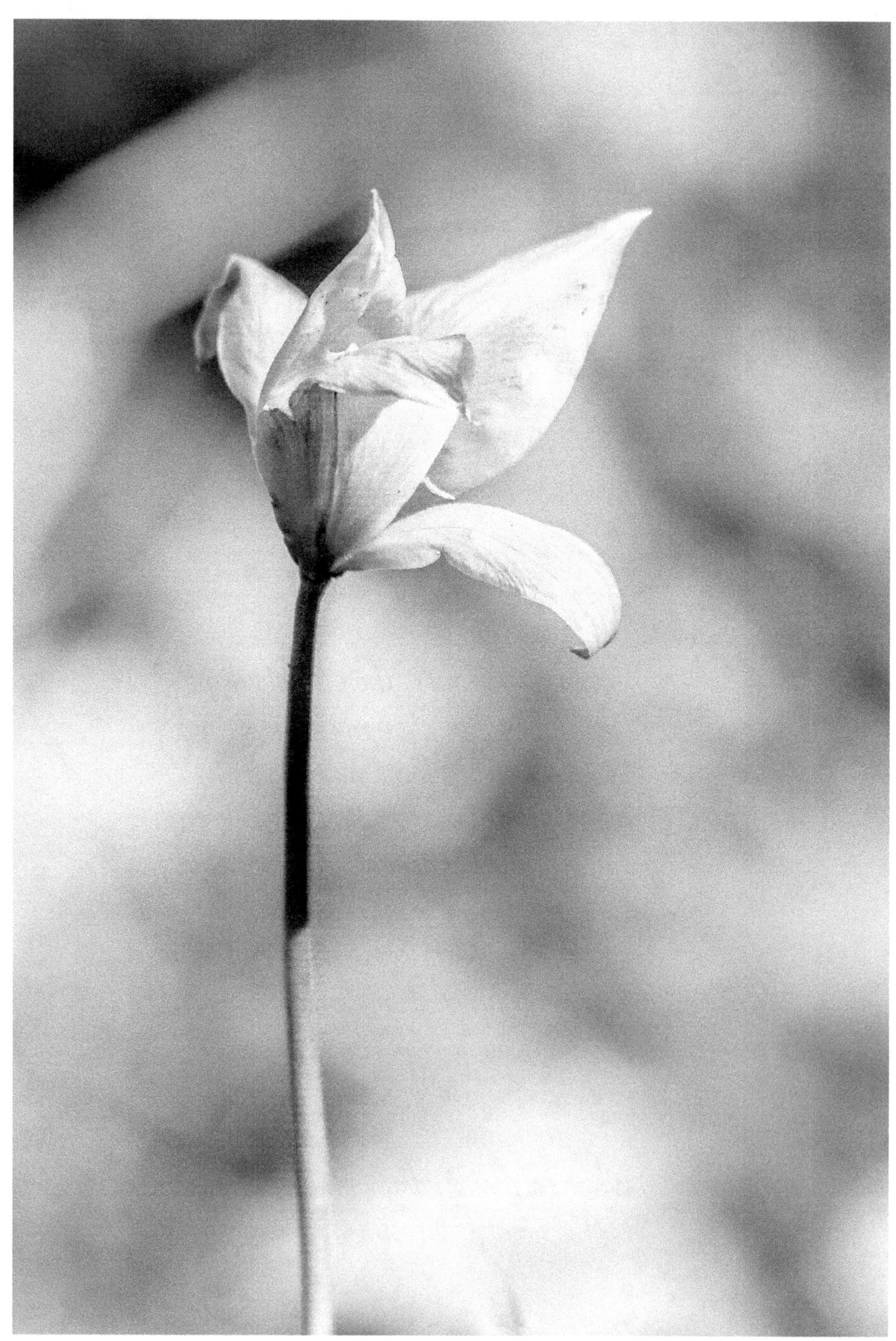

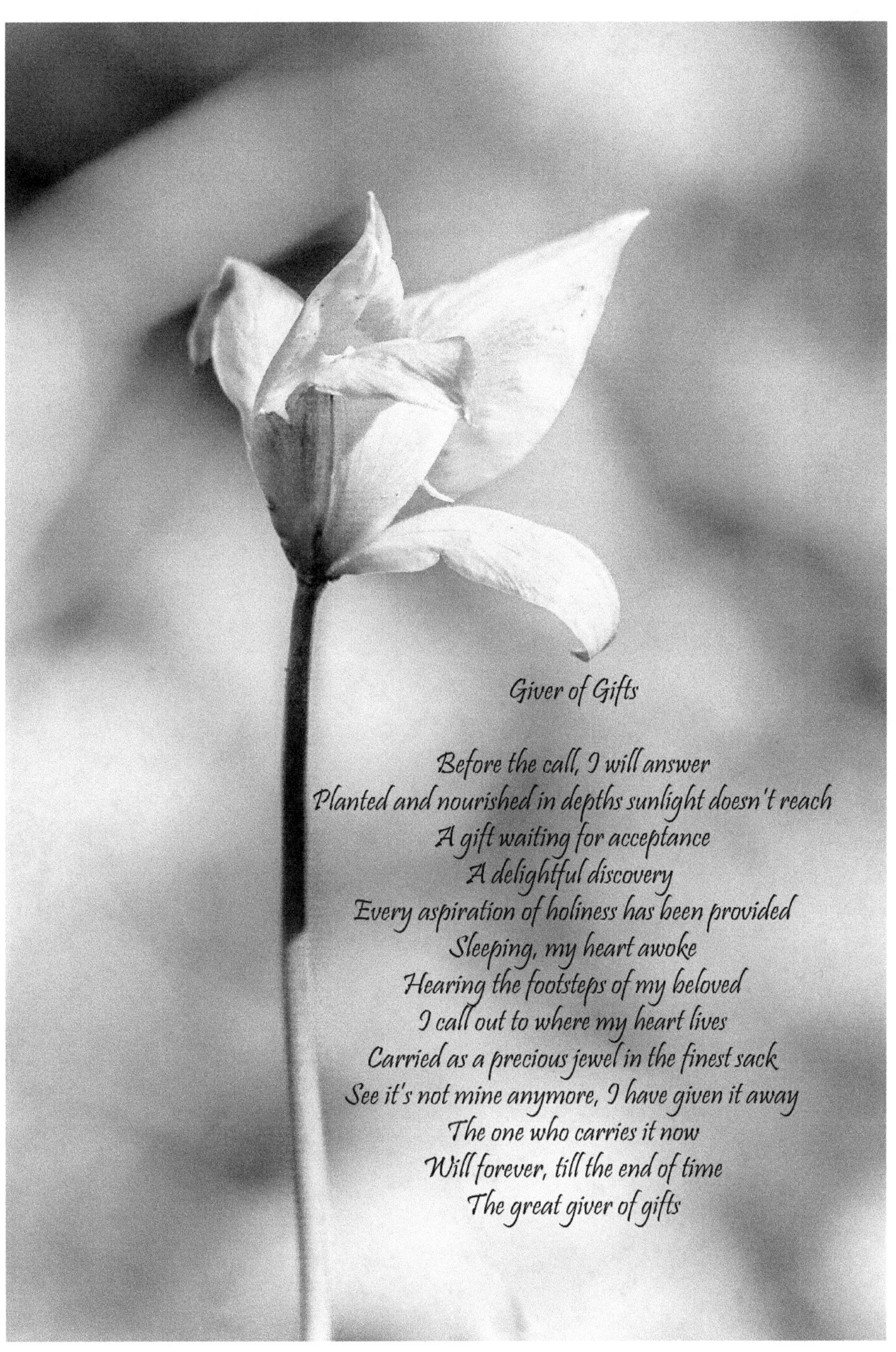

Giver of Gifts

Before the call, I will answer
Planted and nourished in depths sunlight doesn't reach
A gift waiting for acceptance
A delightful discovery
Every aspiration of holiness has been provided
Sleeping, my heart awoke
Hearing the footsteps of my beloved
I call out to where my heart lives
Carried as a precious jewel in the finest sack
See it's not mine anymore, I have given it away
The one who carries it now
Will forever, till the end of time
The great giver of gifts

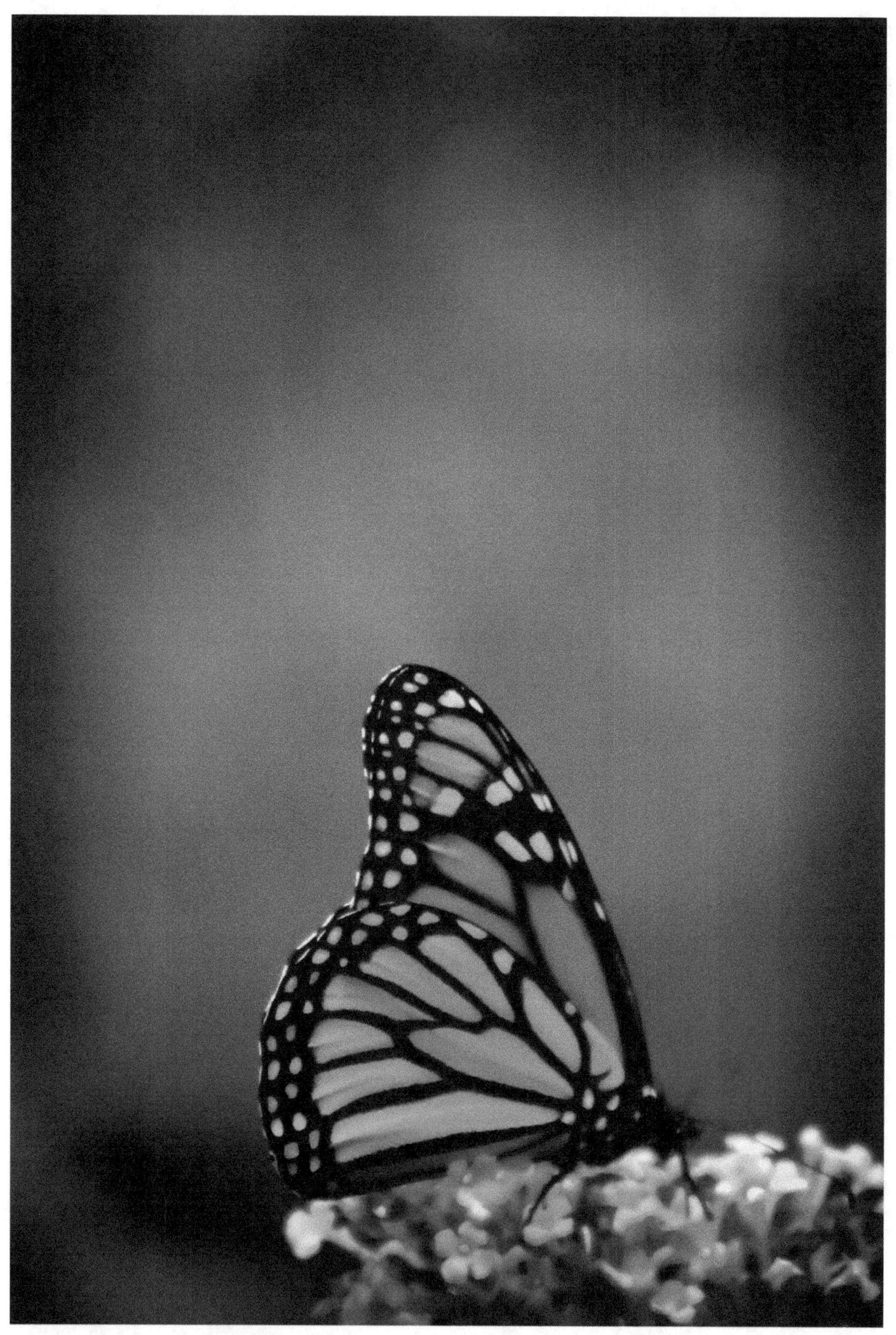

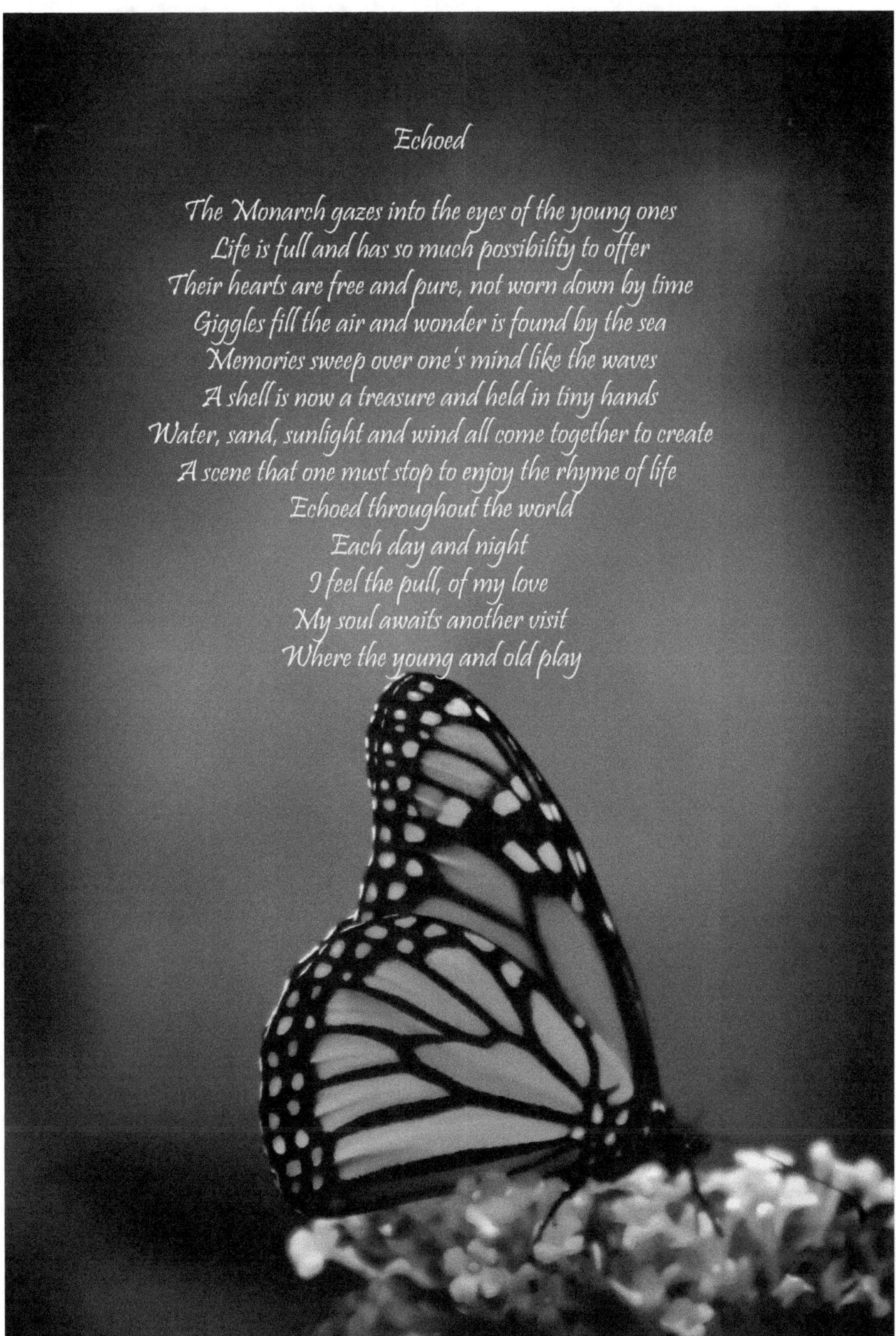
Echoed

The Monarch gazes into the eyes of the young ones
Life is full and has so much possibility to offer
Their hearts are free and pure, not worn down by time
Giggles fill the air and wonder is found by the sea
Memories sweep over one's mind like the waves
A shell is now a treasure and held in tiny hands
Water, sand, sunlight and wind all come together to create
A scene that one must stop to enjoy the rhyme of life
Echoed throughout the world
Each day and night
I feel the pull, of my love
My soul awaits another visit
Where the young and old play

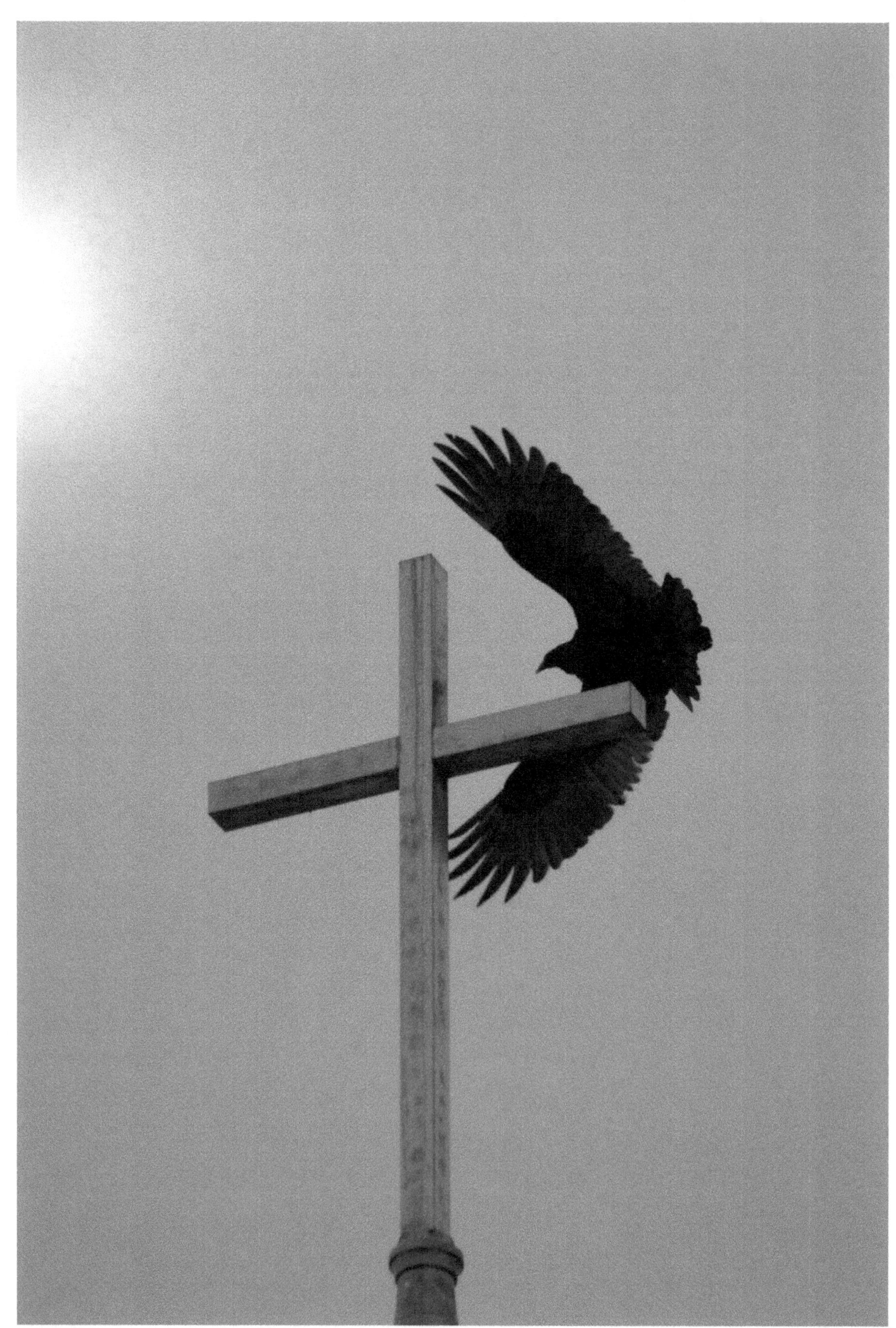

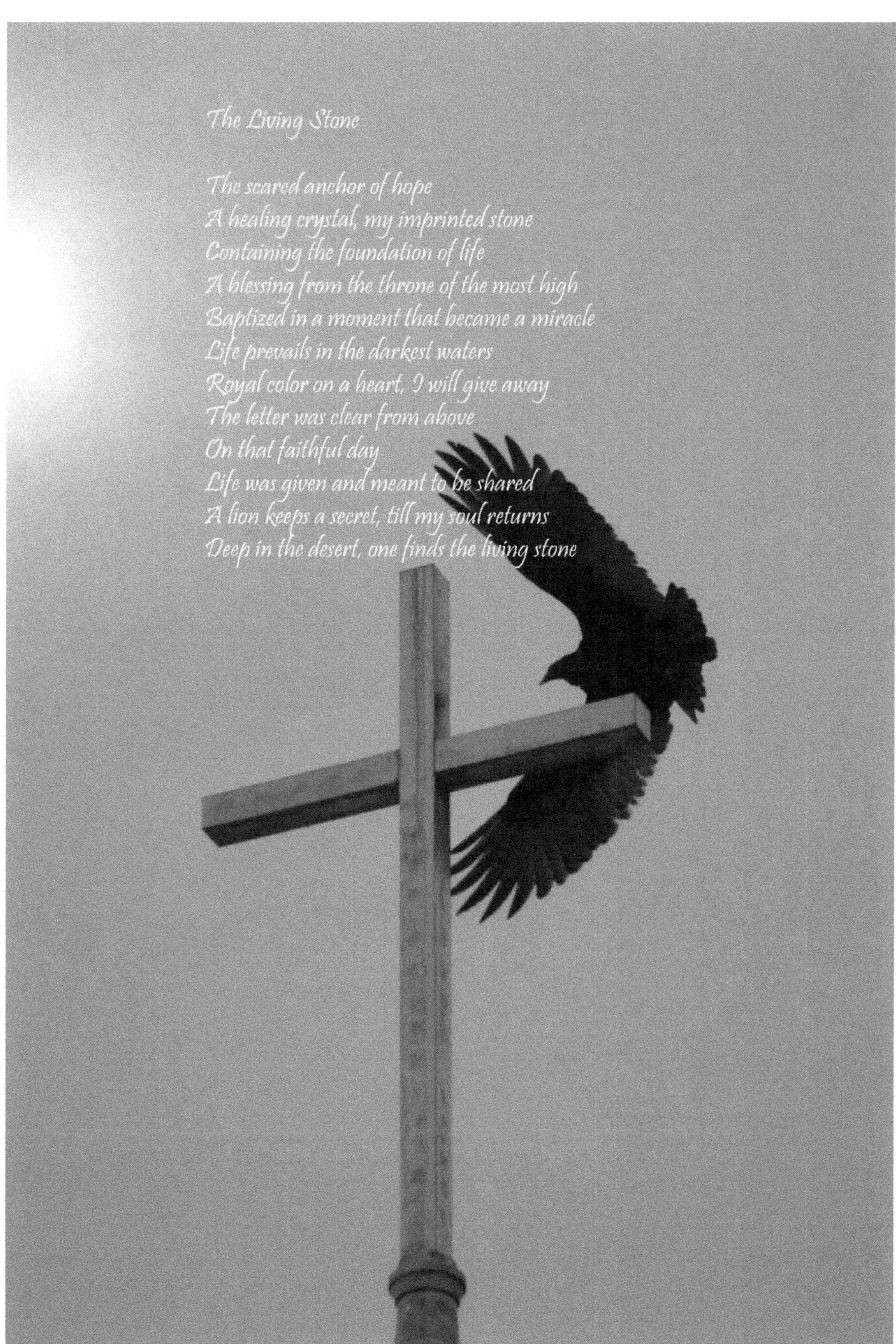
The Living Stone

The scared anchor of hope
A healing crystal, my imprinted stone
Containing the foundation of life
A blessing from the throne of the most high
Baptized in a moment that became a miracle
Life prevails in the darkest waters
Royal color on a heart, I will give away
The letter was clear from above
On that faithful day
Life was given and meant to be shared
A lion keeps a secret, till my soul returns
Deep in the desert, one finds the living stone

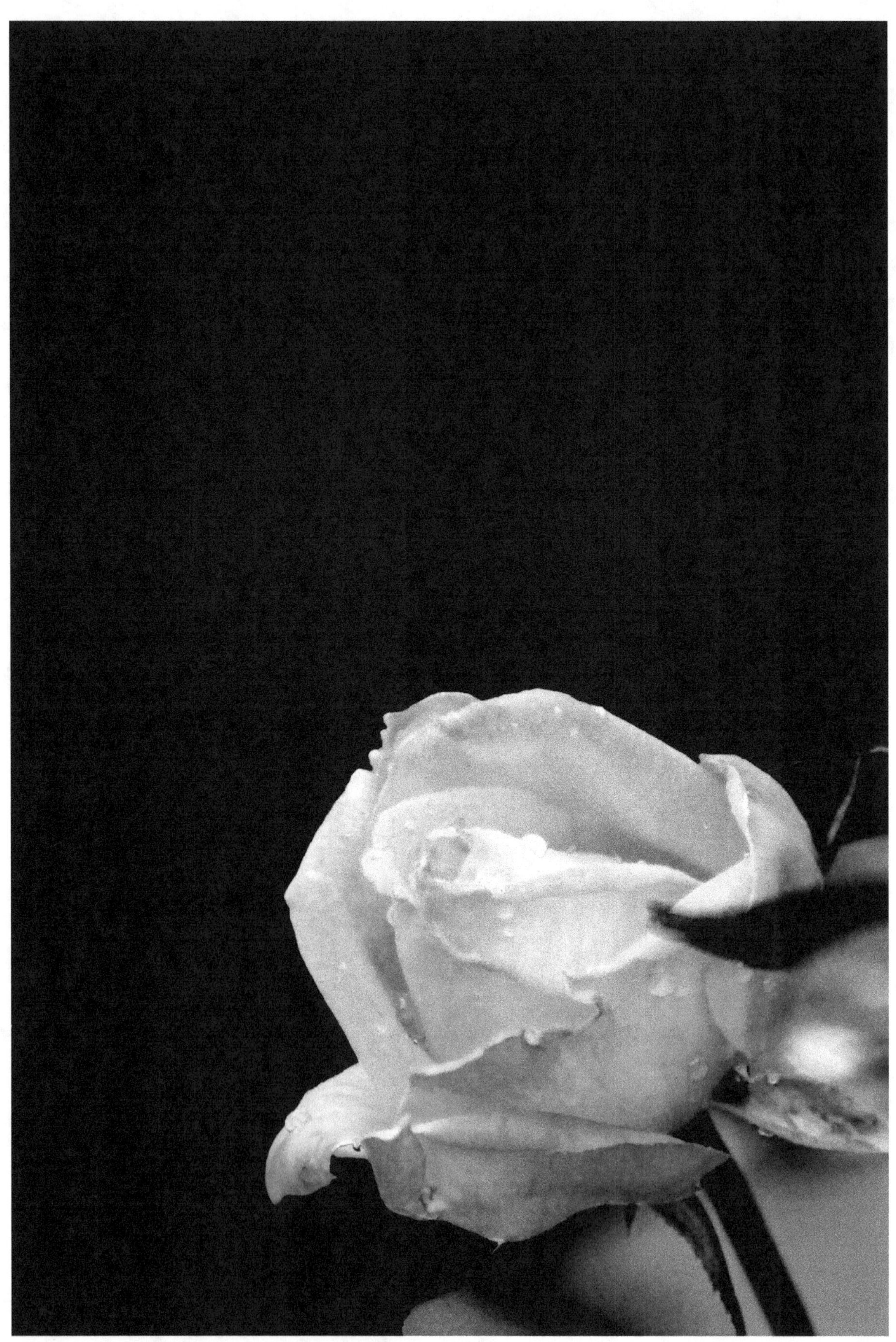

The Band of Gold

I awake to remember the echoes of my mind
Half conscious, the well-known tones aroused the old love
Now the words at last have reached the heart
Listening to them dreamily, recognizing the voice
Love is calling in the gentle tones of affection and desire
Answer, with words of deep tenderness
Bids me to the yearning love shared
A dream of you and I together as one
The band of gold, as we grow old

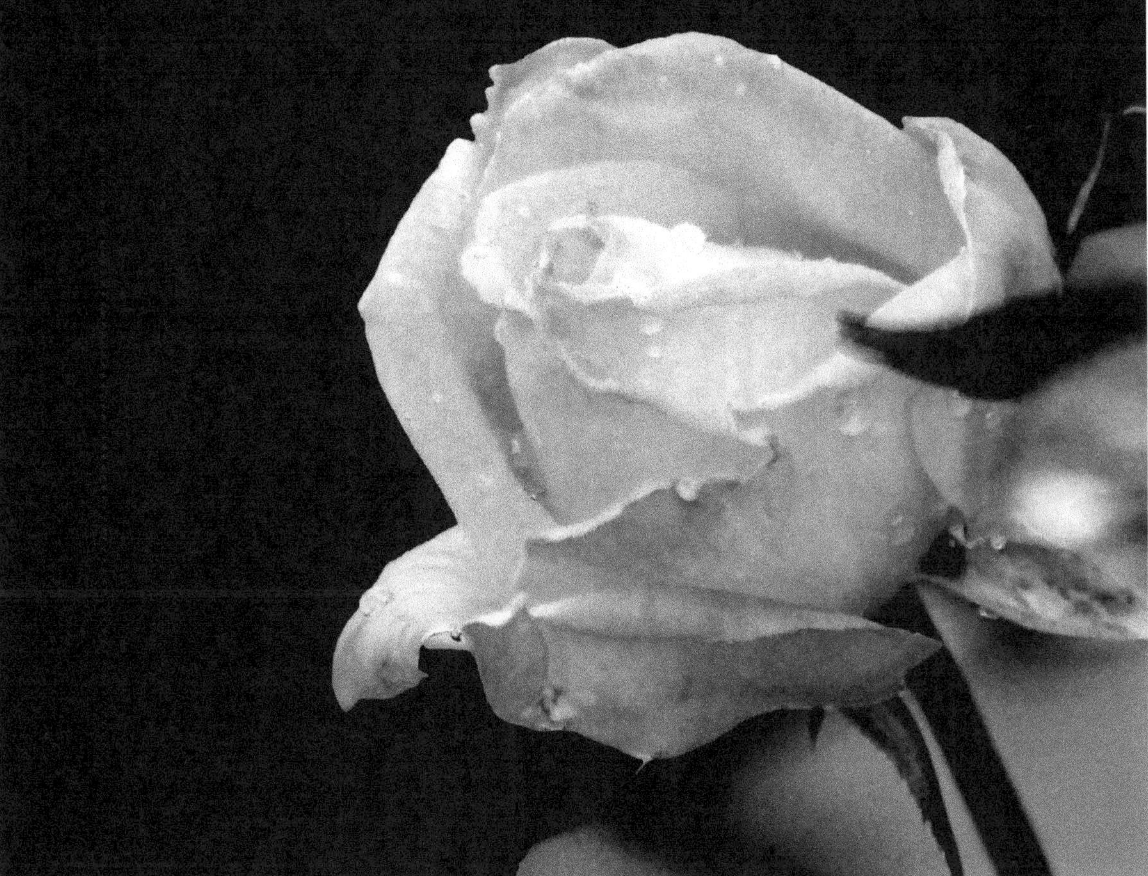

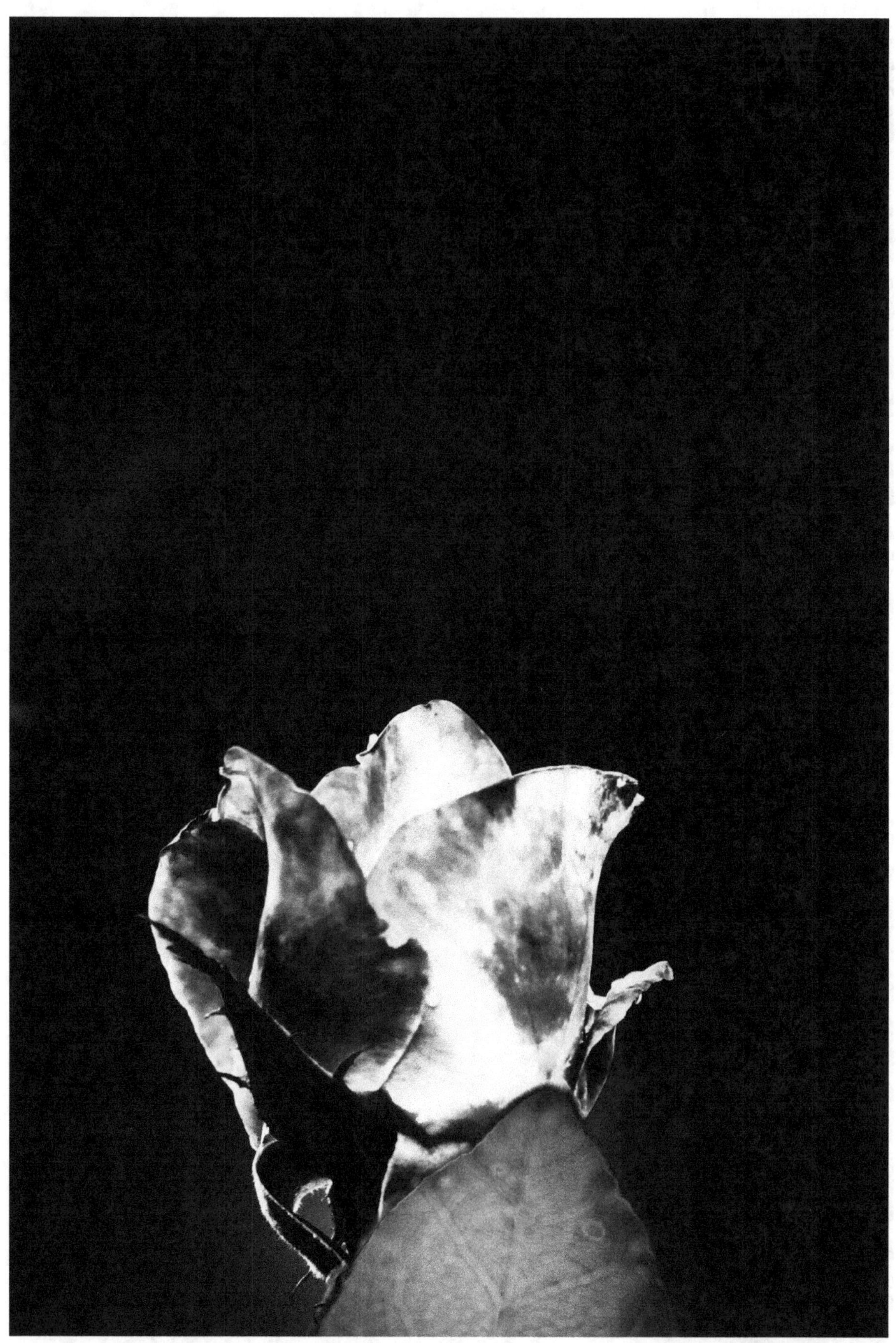

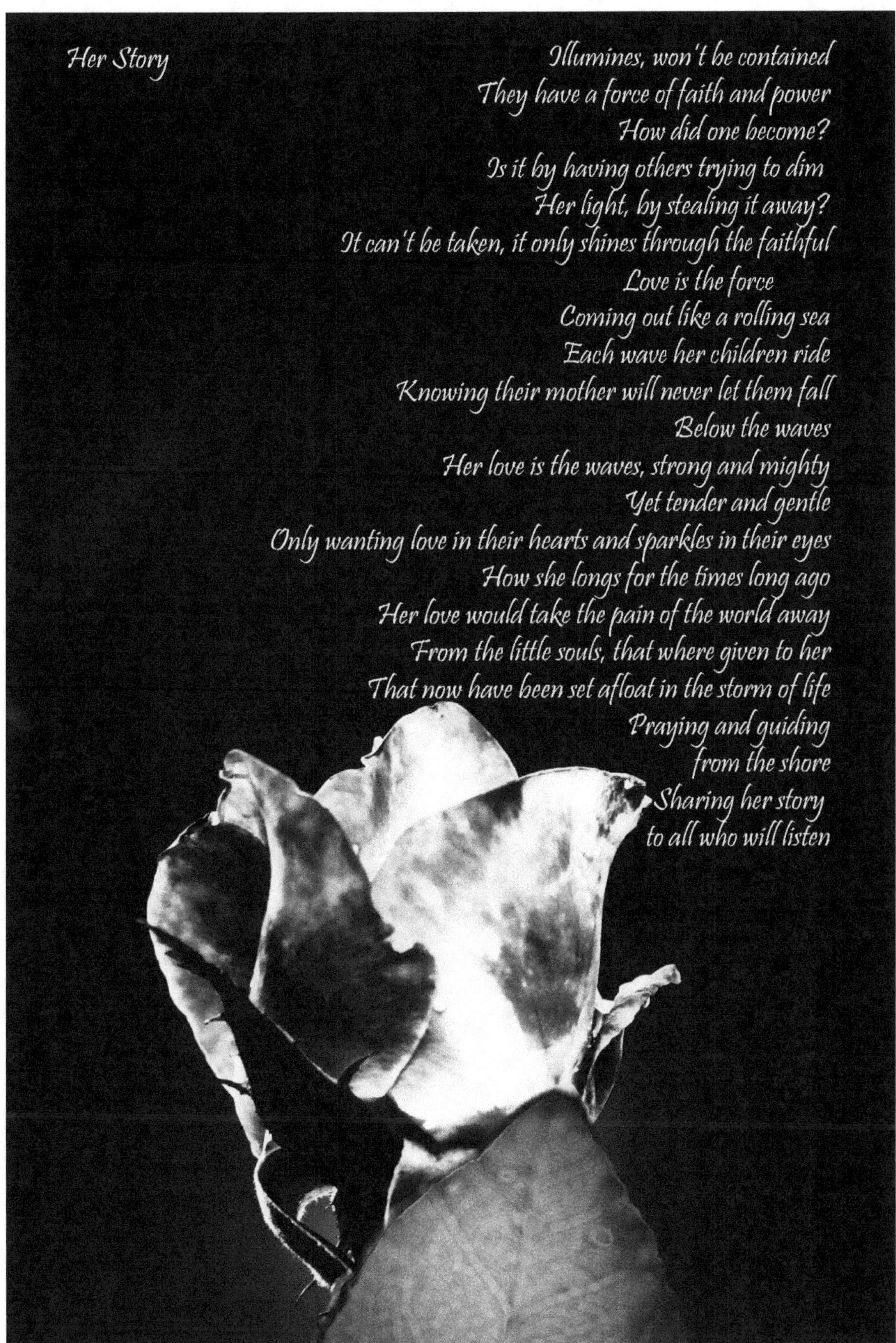
Her Story
Illumines, won't be contained
They have a force of faith and power
How did one become?
Is it by having others trying to dim
Her light, by stealing it away?
It can't be taken, it only shines through the faithful
Love is the force
Coming out like a rolling sea
Each wave her children ride
Knowing their mother will never let them fall
Below the waves
Her love is the waves, strong and mighty
Yet tender and gentle
Only wanting love in their hearts and sparkles in their eyes
How she longs for the times long ago
Her love would take the pain of the world away
From the little souls, that where given to her
That now have been set afloat in the storm of life
Praying and guiding
from the shore
Sharing her story
to all who will listen

www.ingramcontent.com/pod-product-compliance
Lightning Source LLC
LaVergne TN
LVHW061257100826
845148LV00008B/1159
9781614970651